More praise for *Hope Sings*

"Susanna Foth Aughtmon's new book is an invitation to throw off your fears, embrace your most impossible dream, and believe in the God who is singing a song of hope over you. Susanna reminds us, one more time, that our hope is found in the character of the One who spoke the universe into existence with a word and breathed life into the dead. *Hope Sings* is an all-out dare to chase after the life that God has for you. I think you should do it!" —**Mark Batterson**, New York Times best-selling author of *The Circle Maker*, lead pastor of National Community Church

"In true Susanna Foth Aughtmon style, *Hope Sings* had me laughing and crying as she took me on a journey of Hope. I wholeheartedly endorse *Hope Sings* to anyone who wants to be challenged to grow in their faith walk. I found myself relating to her as she vulnerably shared her life. I love the fact that she shares so honestly, yet always points me to Jesus' love and God's enduring Word. It's a winner!" —**Laurie Hoyt**

"*Hope Sings* is written by a storyteller, our daughter Susanna Foth Aughtmon. We are biased, but we love her use of story and metaphor. Writing with a blend of personal experiences, enriched by stories from the Bible, she uses the humor and wisdom that comes from being a pastor's wife and the mother of three sons. Her practical insights inspire readers with the hope that they can sing a song even in the dark of night." —**Dick and Ruth Foth**, authors of *Known: Finding Deep Friendships in a Shallow World*

"In the din of today's fear-mongering world, hope for many seems reduced to a hum. What we need is to be intimately tuned to the One who is Hope, our Lord Jesus. This fresh new book by Susanna Foth Aughtmon does just that. With honest, personal insight, poignant illustrations, and sound biblical teaching, Susanna not only tunes us in but inspires the unbridled courage to give voice to Hope's song and share it with others. I think it's her best book yet, one I will read again and again." —**Judi Braddy**, speaker and author of *Prodigal in the Parsonage, It All Comes Out in the Wash, Everyday Sabbath*, and others

"Hope is like oxygen for our souls. And *Hope Sings* is a deep breath of fresh air. Much of my life and work revolve around the simple idea that there is always hope, no matter the brokenness or injustice. These pages are a refreshing reminder that however dark or long the night, there is always a sunrise." —**Jeremy Vallerand**, president & CEO, Rescue: Freedom International

Risk More • Dream Bigger • Fear Less

Susanna Foth Aughtmon

Abingdon Press
Nashville

HOPE SINGS

RISK MORE. DREAM BIGGER. FEAR LESS.

Library of Congress Cataloging-in-Publication Data has been requested.

ISBN 978-1-5018-2013-7

17 18 19 20 21 22 23 24 25—10 9 8 7 6 5 4 3 2 1

MANUFACTURED IN THE UNITED STATES OF AMERICA

For Scott

You are more than 6'2" on the inside.

My best adventures have been with you.

I love you the most.

Contents

Introduction

Hope is a bright light in the darkness. It is a sun-filled, keep-your-head-up kind of word. It is the belief that, whatever difficulty you are going through at the moment, it is temporary. Better tomorrows are on the way. Hope sweeps in, bringing new life. It lifts us from the pit and strengthens us when we are weak. It gives flight to our dreams and buoys us when we feel like we are sinking in despair. Tertullian, an early church father, said, "Hope is patience with the lamp lit."[1]

We all need hope. Hope for today and more for the future, when life is unknown and uncertain. This book is for the hopeful. For those who shine the light. For those who believe that love conquers all and saves the day in one fell swoop. It is for glass-half-full type of people and for optimists. For those who see the good in each day and consider it their mission to encourage others. Hope is for the ones who see the weary and wounded and cry out, "Hold on! The good stuff is coming!"

This book is for the believers and the faithful. The ones who have tasted grace and have been back for seconds. This book is for the ones who protect hope in its small beginnings, like a newly lit spark, shielding it from the harsh winds and rain of real living, all the while blowing the breath of truth and freedom upon it until it glows and warms everyone that surrounds it.

This book is also for those who have sat in the dark. For those who are wrapped in fear and cloaked in anxiety. It is for those who have longed for a kind word, a good friend, and a decent break. This book is for those who have known despair and dreamt of the dawn. It is for the glass-half-empty type of people, for the pessimists and the naysayers. It is for those who say things like, "Life is hard" and "It can never be done." And this book is for those who have cried their eyes out and then some. For those who have lost once and lost again. This book is for the disappointed. The ones who have lost faith, shaking their fists at the sky, all the while hoping they will be proven wrong. This book is for the ones who need a song in the night. A small wavering tune of hope that lifts the soul and the eyes toward heaven. A song of deliverance. An angel chorus on a cold night out in the middle of nowhere.

This book is for people like you and me. For those who have had moments of great joy and deep darkness. The ones who have watched the news and felt buried by the sorrows of this world. The ones who have kissed the feather-soft lips of a newborn baby and wept for the sheer unadulterated joy of new life. For those who have been both the naysayer and life lover. I have stood with a foot in each camp. Dark and light. Fear and hope. Sorrow and joy. And I have found that the hope side is the better side to be on. It is the side that rejuvenates, regenerates, and heals. If you can find your way to that side? Stay there.

But for those of you who are, in this moment, surrounded by night, who have been set down in a dark place and are circled by despair? There is only one thing left to do. Throw back your head and sing. Because hope has a way of squeezing its way into a song. It sneaks into the melody and brings peace along riding piggyback. It colors each warbled note with reminders of grace and mercy. And when hope sings, it is an invitation for God to come in with all His brightness. Into the dark. Into the sorrow. Into the mess. Light. Life. Love. Hope incarnate. So let the singing begin.

The people who sat in darkness
have seen a great light.
And for those who lived in the land where death casts it shadow,
a light has shined.

Matthew 4:16

CHAPTER 1
Sitting in the Dark

But faith is not necessarily, or not soon, a resting place.
Faith puts you out on a wide river in a boat, in the fog, in the dark.

Wendell Berry

Sitting in the Dark

When I was a child, life was good and simple. I was born in Urbana, near the University of Illinois, to pastor parents. Living in a university town had its perks. Its diverse ethnic culture was married with rural values. College football reigned supreme (Go, Illini, Go!), and the circus stopped by each spring. It was pretty much an idyllic setting. We Foth kids were surrounded by love and good friends and sweet corn. If we were lucky, we got to share the chocolate bars Mom stashed in her purse, and Dad would wrestle with us when he got home from the church at night.

We played hard every day, mostly outside. There wasn't much to be afraid of. Even when the bully down the street tried to take our bikes, we knew Dad would get them back. Our days fell into a rhythm of church on Sundays and school on weekdays. My siblings and I attended Yankee Ridge Elementary about three blocks from our house. We walked there every day and came home to a hot lunch served by Mom. Our teachers were kind, and our classmates were the kids that lived down the street from us. It was just the way life was.

We loved Yankee Ridge. I especially loved my kindergarten teacher, Mrs. Miles, with the wavy blonde hair and shiny shoes. I tried very hard to learn my numbers and listen in class. Those who did were rewarded with one of her kind smiles. As Yankee Ridge students, we got to participate in special activities, like macramé and gymnastics. Every so often, different graduate students from the U of I would come to our elementary school and conduct studies for their doctoral programs. They used us as guinea pigs to prove or disprove their theses. We didn't mind because it got us out of class. One day when I was in kindergarten, I was sent home with a note pinned to my shirt. Teachers didn't do e-mail or texts in the olden days. They safety-pinned important messages to our turtlenecks. I was invited to be a part of a study researching if children were afraid of the dark.

My dad was sitting at the dining room table when he read the note. He asked me, "Are you afraid of the dark?" And I said, "No." Because I was out of preschool, for goodness sake. Of course I wasn't afraid of the dark. I was pretty fearless in my younger years. I knew nothing of the horrors of junior high that awaited me. My dad said, "Do you want to be in the study group to see if you are afraid of the dark?" "Sure." Only babies were scared of the dark. My dad signed the note, I took it back to my teacher, and I was in.

The next day, I was ushered into a small room with a child-sized table and chairs. There were no windows in the room. I was seated at the table, and the grad student told me, "I am going to turn out the light and go outside of the room and shut the door. I want you to see how long you can sit in the dark by yourself." He pointed to the light switch on the wall. "If you get scared, you can turn on the light any time you want. But why don't you try to see how long you can sit in the dark without turning on the light?" I said, "OK." He proceeded to flip off the light and walk out the door, shutting it behind him. It was pitch black. I could no longer see the white-and-gray-flecked linoleum beneath my feet. I took a deep breath, and I sat in the dark. By myself. For all of three seconds. And then I got up and turned the light back on.

The grad student must have been able to tell that the light was back on because he immediately opened the door and came back in the room. He had a perplexed look on his face. "You turned on the light." I nodded. "I thought you said that you weren't afraid of the dark." "I'm not," I answered, confidently. "Then why did you turn the light back on?" Now I was the one looking perplexed. I looked at him and said, "Because I wanted to." Apparently, this guy wasn't the sharpest tool in the shed. He should have known. Given the choice, no one likes to sit in the dark. Especially by themselves. It doesn't take a research paper to figure that out.

Faith in the Dark

You may be wondering what sitting in the dark has to do with hope. All of our greatest hopes spring from our deep well of faith, a belief that the God of the Universe loves us and has a good plan for us. Without faith in a loving and caring God, there is no hope. The problem is that having faith can feel a whole lot like being a kindergartener sitting in the dark. Trusting God with our lives does not come easily. It is hard. And it goes against human nature to do hard things. The dark isn't really our thing. We are lights-on kind of people.

Faith:
Belief. Confidence. Conviction.

But the God of the Universe, the One who created us from dust and breathed life into every living creature, is inviting us on a lights-out adventure. An adventure in the dark that He has designed specifically with us in mind. He is asking us to jump feet first into a story we don't know the ending to. It says in Hebrews 11:1, "Now faith is confidence in what we hope for and assurance about what we do not see" (NIV).

So if we are seeing it, we can be pretty sure that faith is not involved. The Apostle Paul follows up these thoughts in Hebrews 11:6, reminding us, "And without faith it is impossible to please God, because anyone who comes to him must believe that he exists and that he rewards those who earnestly seek him" (NIV).

We desperately want to live a life that is pleasing to Him. We were created for a life of pleasing Him. The internal shift is that most of us came to faith out a life of pleasing ourselves. Before we know Jesus, our bodies, minds, souls, and spirits are completely focused on our own selfish desires. We called all the shots. We didn't care about God or His plans. We only cared about ourselves and our plans. What we didn't know is that the self-pleasing life we were living was leading us down a self-destructive path toward death. Self-centered living always has the same outcome. Before Jesus, we destroyed ourselves with our coveting and hatred and lust. Before Jesus, we drowned ourselves in anger and bitterness. Before Jesus, we were lost in a different kind of darkness—the kind that left us paralyzed in fear and alone with our pain. We were dying moment by moment. We needed saving from the dark. From ourselves.

And that is why Jesus intervened on our behalf. He died so that we could be free from ourselves. He shattered the gates of hell with His powerful love. He showed up with His all-encompassing forgiveness and a new way of living. He brought His healing touch and His truth to our broken spirits. And then He said, "Follow me"(Matthew 4:19 NIV). Follow Me. It is the invitation to faith. It is the clarion call of hope. Follow Me. Leaving the old selfish life behind. Follow Me. Running toward the freeing grace of the One who created us to walk with Him. It is an easy choice if you really think about it. Heads thrown back, arms open wide, we spend our life chasing after Him with all that we are worth, yielding every inch of ourselves to Jesus. We are His—heart, mind, soul, and spirit. We shout at the top of our lungs, "You are in charge. Wherever You are going, that's where I am going! You call the shots from here on out." With faith, we choose the life of yielding everything. At least, we try really hard to choose it. But sometimes those old, selfish thoughts creep in. The ones that make us want to flip on the lights, take control, and forge our own destiny without giving Him and His plans a second thought. It is a daily—or hourly—struggle for some of us walking out our faith.

> *This day I call the heavens and the earth as witnesses against you that I have set before you life and death, blessings and curses. Now*

choose life, so that you and your children may live.

Deuteronomy 30:19 NIV

Amy's Story

Amy lay in bed, her gray hair flattened against the pillow. Her eyes closed, she prayed. Her body was aching and tired even though she had just woken up. But it was a new day. The heat of the rising Tamil Nadu sun pierced through the window. A tiny breeze tugged at the gauzy curtain. The children of the Starry Cluster, those little ones that she and her coworkers had taken in at the Dohnavur Fellowship, would be eating breakfast soon. Their sounds of play would fill the garden. These are the children that had been rescued from temple prostitution, poverty, and a life of slavery. When she arrived in India, she had been an evangelist, sharing the good news. She hadn't known this house, this fellowship, would be her life's work. A mother to the motherless. A teacher. A writer. A songstress.

All she knew when she had left her home in Belfast, Ireland, so long ago was that she wanted to follow Jesus. She wanted to share the love that He had for her with those who were less fortunate than herself. She thought her calling was to Japan. And it had been for a short time. But here she was fifty years later in the land of the mountain tea plantations and steamy jungles. She had never returned home. She spent herself—her heart, soul, mind, and body—in this chosen place. Her hands were gnarled with arthritis, but her heart still beat for the work He had prepared in advance for her to do.

Amy Carmichael sat up in bed, pulling paper and pen from the stand near her bed. She met the day head on. For the past twenty years, she had been an invalid, but there was still work to do. Prayers to be prayed. People to be encouraged. And letters to be written. Picking up where she left off, the nib of the pen scratched against the starchy white paper.[1]

> Some of you who are longing to live this life still hesitate. There is no life in all the world so joyful. It has pain in it too but looking back, I can tell you truly that there is far more joy than pain. Do not hesitate. Give yourselves wholly to Your Lord to be prepared for whatever work he has chosen for you to do later.[2]

As far as Amy was concerned, faith in the One who loved her most of all was the only way. Trusting in the dark. Even when it didn't turn out the way she thought it would. Even when she didn't know what was coming next. Even when old bones ached and writing was a painful chore. Somehow, in His presence. The joy just kept on coming.

Who among you fears the LORD
and obeys the word of his servant?
Let the one who walks in the dark,
who has no light,
trust in the name of the LORD
and rely on their God.

Isaiah 50:10 NIV

Choosing Faith

Jesus wants us to choose life over death. Growth over destruction. Adventure over fear. He wants us to choose life with Him calling the shots. Even in the dark. Even when it seems crazy. No matter what that looks or feels like. In reality, the path that He has for us may not be all that common or sensible. Sometimes He has wild ideas about going into all the world and preaching the gospel. Or being kind to our enemies. Or giving away all our possessions to feed the poor. When we feel Jesus tugging on our heart to go a certain way that doesn't fall in line with common sense (*how do you pay your bills when you have given all your cash to the widows and orphans?*), we worry. *How can this be right?*

It is right because we are leaping into a Spirit-led adventure where His righteousness covers all the bases. His plan has us being solely reliant on Him. He shapes the path of our life according to His perfect will. It is not just our good choices or our common sense that chart the best course for us. It is our belief in the sovereignty of a Holy God and His spectacular plan for our existence that finally gets us moving on the journey we were created for. It is in that moment of committing to a dark river ride in the fog that we actually embrace faith. It is in that place of trust that we launch ourselves, hearts pounding, toward hope.

When we follow the One who loves us most of all into the unknown, into that unseen place where we have to lean on Him and His love and His direction for everything that we need, our adventure begins. Throughout history, He has called his children to follow Him on a lights-out adventure. He called Abraham into the wilderness. He sent Joseph to Egypt. He asked Rahab to leave all that she knew. Our adventure begins with Him calling us to follow Him away from the comfortable life that we know. Because we can't become who we are destined to be, if we are depending on ourselves. Faith requires our total dependence on Him. Every moment of every hour of every day.

We are here to live holy, loving, lowly lives. We cannot do this unless we are walking very, very close to our Lord Jesus.

Amy Carmichael

The Real Question

The real question is: *Are we ready to risk everything that we know for the life we were made for? Are we ready to follow Jesus even when we have no idea where He is going to take us next?* I think the answer is yes. Yes. We are up for it. We may not be Abraham or Joseph or Rahab or Amy Carmichael. We may not establish an entire people group or rule a nation or be a great-great-grandma to a king. We may not be listed with the greats in the faith chapter in Hebrews. We may not be a missionary with a heart for India. But we all long to be the person we were created to be.

We know in our gut that we want in on whatever God has for us. Whatever that life is, wherever it takes us, whoever we become in the process, we want in on faith. The moment we decided to follow Jesus, this desire for deeper faith was birthed in us. And with each small decision to follow, to listen, and to obey the One who loves us most of all, our faith begins to grow.

When you get to the end of all the light you know, and it's time to step into the darkness of the unknown, faith is knowing that one of two things shall happen: either you will be given something solid to stand on, or you will be taught how to fly.

Edward Teller

Faith is what we are made for. So what if we can't see? So what if we have no idea what is coming next? This place of faith and believing in the God of the Universe? This is when we get to see miracles and hear answered prayers and live out stories that we are going to get to tell our children and our children's children. We may not be able to see where we are going, but we can know if we are following the One who loves us most of all? It is about to get good.

Faith is jumping feet first into a story you don't know the ending to.

CHAPTER 2

Faith and Fear

I am not afraid of storms, for I'm learning how to sail my ship.

Louisa May Alcott

The Comfort Zone

My comfort zone is reading a book on the couch, surrounded by my family, sipping a creamy cup of coffee. My uncomfort zone? Standing in front of a large group of people, speaking and drawing attention to myself. I would call this my now-is-when-I-really-start-sweating zone. After my first book came out, I started receiving invitations to speak at churches and retreats and moms' groups. I couldn't help thinking, *Don't they know that writers write about their feeling so they don't have to actually stand up and TALK them?* Life is funny that way. You think that you are at your best in your comfort zone. And God thinks, "You are comfortable in your comfort zone. You are at your best when you trust Me."

My friend Mark, pastor of National Community Church, e-mailed me and invited me to come speak in Washington D.C. for Mother's Day around this time. He invited me to speak three times in one weekend. My husband, Scott, and I had been on staff with Mark and his wife, Lora, for a year and a half before embarking on planting a church on the San Francisco peninsula. We love those people more than words can say. How fun would it be to hang out with them? I messaged him, "Yes! We would love to come." Then he e-mailed me again and said, "And let's do a women's event on Saturday, too." I knew that this was an opportunity that God had ordained for me. I have always told myself I won't let my fear hold me back. Why was I sweating while reading an e-mail?

I wrote him back, "Sounds good!" And then I put my head down on my kitchen table and wept. For a solid ten minutes. Because of all the terror that was welling up within me. What if I failed? What if I was a horrible speaker? What if I embarrassed Mark and myself? What if I couldn't articulate what God was putting on my heart? What if the Holy Spirit checked out during my talk, and no one got a morsel of goodness from it? Or even worse, what if I wasn't funny? Because clearly, that is the most important thing of all. My heart was pounding, and I felt a little nauseous. I was three months out from the actual speaking engagement, and I was showing early signs of cardiac arrest. Sweet Jesus, help me now.

Funny thing . . . sometimes the doors that God opens for us feel like the door that the Road Runner used to open for Wile E. Coyote in the cartoons. You know, the one that led off a cliff into nothingness. Now, I know that is super disheartening to hear. But it is the truth. God isn't opening scary doors because He doesn't like us. He doesn't want us to take a leap of faith just so that we can fall flat on our face. God opens doors of opportunity and risk because He knows who we are and who He created us to be. He sees our fear and says, "Now let's get rid of that." How do we get rid of our many and varied fears, you ask? By facing them. By walking into them. By looking them straight in the eye. So much for comfort zones.

Here is the problem that God has with comfort zones. Yours and mine. We love them so much we don't ever want to leave them. We are so desperate to find those places in life with no stress, no conflict, and no risk that once we do find them, we just want to stay put. We want to stop following His lead. Most of us try to find as many ways as possible to be comfortable. We want comfortable families, comfortable churches, and comfortable jobs. Being comfortable doesn't hurt. It feels safe and good and right. But there is very little faith involved in being comfortable. Our comfort is usually found in the relief and solace from a wild world. Our faith usually calls us out *into the wild world* and challenges us to do impossible things in impossible circumstances. This is where God does His best work.

Faith is to believe what you do not see,
the reward of this faith is to see what you believe.
Saint Augustine

The Faith Adventure

I have heard Mark say on many occasions, "If you're bored, one thing is for sure: you're not following in the footsteps of Christ." Faith and boredom don't mix. Comfort is rarely a factor in faith. And for your faith to actually grow, you are going to need to take risks and dream big dreams, and you are going to need to be brave. Some of us think, *Well, if you can guarantee me that everything will turn out the way I want it to, I will take some more risks.* Here's the thing with faith: there are no money-back guarantees. Actually, I'm wrong. There are two guarantees that you will find on your faith journey. Here they are:

Your life will most likely not go exactly the way that you want it go.
and
You will be scared.

Fear has a way of rearing its ugly head when you are in the dark.

Grown-up Fears

Being afraid when you are a child is normal. But fear can follow you into adulthood, too. When I was a sophomore in college, the Loma Prieta earthquake hit our college campus in Northern California. My dad was the president of the small college I attended. Tucked up in foothills of the Santa Cruz Mountains, the heavily wooded campus was located three miles from the epicenter of the quake. My parents lived close to the campus, and I was at home with my family when the earthquake hit. We felt every ripple of that seismic event. It was a 6.9 on the Richter scale and shook us to our cores. It shook us so hard, we thought Jesus was coming back.

Our house was rocking so violently that I fell into the bathroom when I tried to stand in its door way. I heard my Mom saying, "Jesus, Jesus!" over and over again. My brother, Chris, a daredevil at heart, was even praying out loud. This quake was no joke. It wreaked havoc in the surrounding towns, damaging buildings and leaving the county without electricity for nearly a week. Our college advised everyone to go home until the campus was back up and running. But my home was also without electricity. I was traumatized by the 5.0 aftershocks we kept having. I decided to go home with my cousin, Beth, to her house in Modesto, about an hour and a half away.

We hitched a ride to Beth's house with some friends. On the drive to Modesto, they were playing a Christian radio show during which the host was interviewing an allegedly demon-possessed person. The guest was quarrelsome. (Helpful hint: Interviewing demons? Not a good call.) There was a lot of growling going on during the interview. It was an unnerving ride to say the least. I would have preferred listening to something a little more on the light side. Maybe some soft jazz to soothe our already-frayed nerves? But it wasn't our car, so we endured. We got to Beth's house late that night. Uncle John and Aunt Neva were already in bed, so we let ourselves in and climbed in bed.

We were just drifting off to sleep when we heard it. The worst sound I have ever heard in my life. There was a ragged scratching sound coming from the screen outside Beth's window. It was a kind of plucking sound, like bone against wire. The kind of sound you would expect to come from a demon's finger. We didn't say anything. We could barely breathe. We lay paralyzed in the dark. In the pitch blackness of that room, with only the sound of our quickened breathing accompanying the nerve-wracking sound of twanging window screen, I was convinced that the demon-possessed radio guest had come to call.

All of a sudden, Beth yelled out into the midnight air, "YOU GUYS BETTER CUT IT OUT!" She slid out from the bed onto the floor. I, however, couldn't move. Laid out flat with fear, I was mostly weeping. Great tears rolled from my eyes, soaking my pillow. This was it. We had made it through the earthquake, and now we were going to die. Clearly, the demoniac had sensed us through the radio speakers in the car and had found us with some sort of evil GPS.

You may be thinking, *Why didn't you just turn on the lights?* Are you crazy? We weren't going to let the sicko outside know where we were. We were kept safe under a cover of darkness. Beth is a small woman, but she is not one you would want to mess with. As Shakespeare would say, "Though she be but little, she is fierce."[1] In all her fierceness, as I was lying there and crying my eyes out, she had the forethought to call Uncle John on the phone. (She had a separate phone line in her room.) In moments, Uncle John was in the room flipping on the lights and throwing open the shade. Outside the window stood two of our girlfriends from college, holding an almond tree branch that they had been raking across the window. Needless to say, the relationship was touch and go for a while after that. Fear has a way of shutting things down.

Paralyzed or Galvanized

Fear can shut everything down when it comes to faith, too. Fear can paralyze you, just like it paralyzed me in the bed that night. It can lay you out and keep you from becoming the person that God created you to be. If you let your fear determine your faith, you will never do anything. You will never go anywhere. You will never step out. Following Jesus doesn't mean you will never be scared. In fact, it might be better to think of it this way:

If you aren't a little scared, you might not be living the life you were made for.

Because fear is a normal part of being alive. It is normal to be scared when you are doing something as tremendous, as fantastic, and as risky as following Jesus. And if you aren't a little afraid, you can't be brave.

Being Brave

During World War I, Eleanor Roosevelt was asked by the Red Cross to visit St. Elizabeth's Hospital in Washington, DC. Her husband, Franklin, was the assistant secretary of the Navy. She knew it was her duty to go, but she was terrified. The new artillery that was employed on the battlefield, the grenades, machine guns, and mustard gas were wreaking havoc on the bodies, minds, and spirits of the young recruits. The soldiers who were coming home to this hospital were often seriously wounded and maimed. Many of them were suffering from shell shock or what we now call post-traumatic stress disorder. Some would never recover, their families left to deal with the fallout.

Eleanor didn't know what she would see or what kind of mental wounds she would encounter. She didn't know what to say to the soldiers or how to act, but she felt that in light of how they had served their country, they needed to be loved and cared for, in spite of her fear. She became an advocate for their families, receiving aid and lobbying for humane treatment of the soldiers who were suffering. She didn't let her fears stop her from doing what her heart told her she needed to do.[2] She said, "You gain strength, courage and confidence by every experience in which you really stop to look fear in the face. You must do thing you think that you cannot do."[3]

She let her heart, her passion, her belief in what was right and good galvanize her into action.

Galvanize:
Rouse. Electrify. Animate.

If you are not taking a risk or dreaming big dreams or stepping out in faith, you won't be scared. *You will simply stay where you are and stay who you are.*

But if you are in the middle of walking out your faith adventure, if you have decided to take a risk or dream big dreams, and you are finding yourself scared out of your mind, you should know this: You are in good company. The Bible is full of people who were scared to death to do what God asked them to do. God will always ask us to be more and do more and say more than we can ever be or do or say on our own. It is in those moments of fear, when we are the most dependent on Him, when our belief in who He is and what He can do galvanizes us into action, His glory shines through.

Like Eleanor Roosevelt, we must do the thing we think we cannot do. We can't let fear dictate our actions. We can't let fear determine if or when or how we walk out our faith. There is only one thing we can do. We can remember the words that the Lord spoke through Isaiah to the Israelites:

Don't be afraid, for I am with you.
Don't be discouraged, for I am your God.
I will strengthen you and help you.
I will hold you up with my victorious right hand.

Isaiah 41:10

And then we can do what millions of others of Christ-followers have done before us. We can let fear be our springboard to faith. We can be brave.

Let your fear be the springboard to faith.

CHAPTER 3

Being Brave

Only those who will risk going too far can possibly find out how far one can go.

T. S. Eliot

Crossing Bridges

There is a 984-foot-long, glass-bottom bridge in China that beckons the fearless. It is made of steel cables and three layers of crystal-clear glass and spans a giant rocky crevice.[1] The bridge sways 580 feet above the ground; and while you stand on it, you can see straight down to the bottom of a harrowing gorge. It is called Brave Man's Bridge. It is a good name. But when I showed my son, Jack, a picture of it, he said, "They should call it Dumb Man's Bridge." He has an aversion to heights. I get it. Just looking at the picture makes me want to cry.

People crossing the bridge are fitted with blue cloth booties. They cross it in a variety of ways. Some of them are clutching friends. Some close their eyes and shuffle across, their lips moving silently in prayer. And then there are those who crawl on their hands and knees. Palms on glass, eyes locked on the other end of the bridge, they inch their way across. I recognize the look of panic on their faces because I, too, am a bridge crawler. I have sunk to my knees with the fear of a treacherous crossing. I have sensed the prickle of sweaty fear on the back of my neck. I have felt the splintering timber of a bridge cut into my hands as I faced my destiny. There is no shame in crawling across a bridge. OK, there is a little shame. But who even cares as long as you make it to the other side?

Being Brave Doesn't Have to Look Pretty

I crawled the length of my first bridge during sixth grade. It was a thirty-foot-long giant redwood log spanning the sandy banks of a rain-swollen creek with a five-foot drop. And I felt like I was going to die. I was at science camp in the Santa Cruz Mountains with one hundred sixth-graders from Vine Hill Elementary School. Crowded on one side of the creek were those of us who hadn't crossed. On the other side were the victors. The champions. The triumphant. The bridge crossers. There was no escape. Every student was required to cross the bridge.

Some kids galloped across the log, camp counselors cheering them on. Others picked their way across slowly, arms flung out wide to steady themselves. The shouts of joy echoed up off the canopy of redwood forest each time a student stepped safely to the other side. As the line moved slowly forward, my heart began to pound. I had no idea that I was afraid of crossing bridges until this moment.

Earlier in the day, I had worked my way across a higher portion of the creek on a taut rope line. With hands clinging to one rope at chest level, and my feet balancing on another rope, I shimmied my way across. I was a little nervous, but I wasn't terrified. What scared me the most about the redwood log crossing was that there was nothing to hold on to. Just air. There were no helmets or safety nets. This was the 1980s. As kids, we lived on the brink of death every day.

When I got to the front of the line, my camp counselor grinned and said, "OK, Susanna, you can do it. Let's go." I think she was all of fifteen years old. *What did she know?* Did she know that I was ready to throw up? Did she see tears were gathering at the corners of my eyes? Didn't she know that I was going to totally humiliate myself? I was too much of a people pleaser to say, "No, I will not cross the bridge." And I wasn't a quitter, either. I did what any reasonable person could. I folded at the knees and dropped on all fours, gripping that log like there was no tomorrow. And I began to crawl. I was going to get it done. But I was going to get it done on my terms.

I don't remember anyone laughing. I don't remember anyone cheering when I reached the end of the log. I don't think many at camp opted for crawling. But I know one thing: I made it across. I had done the thing that I thought I could not do. I was brave. But my small act of bravery could not compare with the bravery of another bridge crawler in July of 1881. Kate Shelley took being brave to a whole different level.

Bravery:
Fearlessness. Boldness. Daring. Audacity. Spunk.

The Des Moines River Bridge

When Kate Shelley dropped to her knees on that fateful summer night in 1881, her heart was thundering in her chest. The wind whipped and tore at her dress. Rain pelted her father's railroad lantern in her hand and soaked the old straw hat pressed to her head. Flashes of bright lightning lit the sky, and the roar of the Des Moines River rushed under the bridge, filling her ears. At seventeen, Kate was smart enough to know that crossing this treacherous bridge wasn't the best idea. To cross it during a torrential thunderstorm was sheer madness. To discourage bridge crossers, the railroad company had removed the flooring from between the ties. One misstep would plunge Kate 184 feet below into the rushing river.

Kate wasn't a daredevil, but there was no one else to tell the nearest railroad station that the Honey Creek Bridge was out. Her father had died in a railroad accident when she was twelve. Her mother's health had failed under the strain of that loss. With the midnight express train barreling toward Honey Creek Bridge, there was no time to lose. If the train wasn't stopped, its passengers would jump the tracks and slam into the raging flood waters. Kate had to cross the Des Moines River Bridge. It was her only hope of saving them.

Kate began to crawl. While she clutched at the lantern with one hand, the rough-hewn ties bit into her knees. The wind whistled between the gaps in the bridge as she struggled to maintain her balance. With eyes locked on the end of the bridge, she inched forward, one tie at a time. In the deluge of rain, the lantern sputtered out. Kate crawled the rest of the way across the bridge, blind, using the flashes of lightning as her guide.

Her knees scooting forward and palms clutching the splintered wood, she almost began to weep with relief when she touched the hard-packed dirt at the end of the bridge. Pulling herself to her feet, she ran the length of the track to Iowa's Mongoina Station. Throwing open the door, she alerted the station agent of the looming danger before collapsing, unconscious. He recognized that Kate was a railroad man's daughter. The life-saving message was wired to the next station, and the train was stopped. In a moment that truly mattered, Kate was beyond brave.[2]

The Fearful or the Faithful

Most of us don't choose to put ourselves in situations where we are scared. We don't like feeling like we are out of control or that bad things could happen to us. We don't want to cross bridges. We are not looking to save the day. But there are moments in our lives that, in order to become all that we are destined to be, we have to overcome our fear and be brave. These are bridge moments. We need to get from point A to point B. On our own, we know it is an impossibility. *How can it be done?* Countless times in the Bible, we see people using their fear as a springboard to faith.

Abraham left behind all he knew to establish a new nation. He believed that God would keep His promise and give him more descendants than all the stars in the sky. Joseph embraced a life he never wanted after he was sold into slavery by his own brothers. He believed that the dreams God had given him of ruling a nation would come true. Somehow. Someway. Rahab became a traitor to her own people, hiding the Israelite spies from her government. She believed that because of God's intervention, she and her family would be saved from certain death. They were all brave.

Abraham, Joseph, and Rahab all used their fear to jump off into the wideness of God's grace, the richness of His promises, and the depths of His unexpected goodness. They had to take the proverbial leap of faith. They had to believe. They had to be brave. But when they did, they were met with hope. If fear is the wide chasm that paralyzes us and drops us to our knees, then hope is the bridge that spans every weakness, every heartache, and every pain that keeps us there.

Being brave is a hallmark of faith. It is an indicator of a life given in surrender to a God who is bigger and greater and more amazing than we can ever dream to be. Hope bridges the gap between our fear and God's path for us. It is never God's desire for us to be scared. It is His intention for us to be full up with His presence. His goodness. His light. His love. His peace. His Spirit.

For God has not given us a spirit of fear and timidity,
but of power, love, and self-discipline.

2 Timothy 1:7

God's intention is for us to live out a bold life of faith that is full of purpose. Our humanity keeps us pinned down with fear. But God living within us? The fullness of His grace and mercy buoying us? His strong promises and innate goodness hemming us in on every side? This enables us to overcome fear. Not because we are especially talented or large minded. But because He has infused us with His power, His love, and His self-discipline.

When we get lost in the dark, we tend to forget His plan and His purpose for us. We forget that fear is not from Him. We forget that the One who loves us the most counts our tears. We forget that no matter what the outcome is, we are not alone. In His power, we can do the impossible. Held in His love, we are safe. As His disciples, we are walking in His footsteps and learning His ways.

The truth is that we are bridge people. Some of us are runners, but most of us are crawlers. Palms to the ground, we are choosing to get from point A to point B—no matter what. We are crossing the wide river of fear to that place of peace that only comes when we reach the other side. We are risking it all for the good stuff. We recognize that when we are facing a bridge, we are not at the end of our rope; we are in the middle of our story. And we are clinging with our hands, knees, fingers, and toes to hope.

Hope is a bridge.

CHAPTER 4
The Big Questions

I don't think there are any rude questions.

Helen Thomas

We Have Some Questions

When I was seven years old, we moved from the cornfields of Urbana, Illinois, to Scotts Valley, California. We moved from suburbia to a country road nestled at the foothills of the Santa Cruz Mountains. The twisty road was bordered by horse pastures and hippy enclaves. You turned off of the main road onto a gravelly lane and drove up a steep, winding hill to two houses perched on top. Our house was the house on the right. We went from living in a neighborhood surrounded by kids our age to living in the mountain wilderness. Or at least, that is what it felt like to us. It matched how we felt inside. Wild.

My dad had taken a position as college president of the small Bible college that he and Mom had attended fifteen years earlier. My parents were both Californians by birth. Even though we were moving nearer to grandparents, cousins, aunts, and uncles, we kids were in shock. We hated California. We missed everything about Illinois. Our people. Our places. Our lives. Mom and Dad kept up a brave face. They knew that this was God's next step for them and for us. It had had been confirmed in a dozen different ways. But they were feeling the loss of the close-knit church family they had planted and left behind. Change is never easy, even when it is good.

Our new house was built into the side of the sandstone mountain, surrounded by a wide deck. Some people would have thought it was a serene sanctuary, framed by looming redwoods and fragrant eucalyptus. But we kids felt isolated. We felt upended. We were undone. Our first days of school were traumatic. We were attending three different schools. Erica began her first day of junior high without a friend in sight. Jenny forgot her lunch at drop off and, while sobbing, ran through the sprinklers after Mom's car to get it. Chris screamed and cried when Mom dropped him off and had to be restrained by his first grade teacher. And I felt like I was going to throw up. I had a new teacher and new classmates, and I sat across from a boy at lunch who liked to squish chewed-up banana through his front teeth to gross people out. It worked. I thought he was gross. I thought California was gross. We all just wanted to go back home.

We asked my parents a lot of questions like:

"How long do we have to stay here?"

"Do you think we will ever move back?"

"When can we see our friends?"

"If we have to live in California, why don't we move to Modesto with all of our cousins?"

And the biggest question of all:

"Why did we have to move here in the first place?"

We missed our comfort zone. That place where we were known and loved. When you are a child, it is hard to articulate what you are feeling. You just know you feel sweaty and a little nauseous when your world is changed up on you. You act out in anger. You weep at the drop of a hat. You lash out. You withdraw. You are grappling with the big questions of life. *Why? What? When?* and *Where?* And the reason that you are asking these questions is because you think if you can find the answers, then you will feel more settled in your soul. That the gaping hole of hurt will go away with the right answers. Asking questions is how you figure out the world around you. It is the reasonable response to encountering something that you can't comprehend or understand. If you are asking questions, you are on the right path.

Question:
Inquiry. Investigation. Examination.

All of Our Wonders

We were built for asking questions. Anyone who doubts this has never been around a two-year-old. The word *question* comes from the Latin word *quarere,* which means "search or inquiry" and is the same root word for "quest."[1] Every important discovery on this earth has sprung from the end of a question mark. All of humanity is on a quest. The world around us is a wonder-full place to be explored and discovered. *Why? What? When? How?* The words shape the world that we live in today. Whether you are an explorer, pioneer, farmer, pastor, teacher, engineer, scientist, or philanthropist, your learning voyage begins with a question:

Is the world round?
Is there a cure for cancer?
Can humans fly?
What kind of land is over that mountain?
How can I best teach my students?
How do I connect to God?
Can I help the world be a better place?

These questions are based on wonder. They are the launching pad that fling us out into new directions as we risk, dream, hope, and hope some more. Questions launch us into uncharted territory. They shape the way that we act and think. We go looking for answers to the world's questions, and our world begins to change.

But there are other questions, too. The ones that spring from the well of doubt that each of us drinks from as members of humanity. The ones that we ask when we are scared and hurt. They leap into our hearts and minds when our reality is too much for us to take in. Following God and His path does not allow us to escape the troubles of this world. We struggle. We doubt. We wrestle. We ask hard questions like:

What if I fail?
Why is my life turning out this way?
Why am I in so much pain?
Why is this situation so difficult?
Is this all I am ever meant to be?
Why is there so much grief and disappointment surrounding me?
When will I get out of this mess that I am in?
Why is life so hard if I am doing what God called me to do?
Will it ever be different?
How can I do something I have never done before?
How can I be someone I have never been before?

Can a mortal ask questions which God finds unanswerable? Quite easily, I should think. All nonsense questions are unanswerable. How many hours are in a mile? Is yellow square or round? Probably half the questions we ask—half our great theological and metaphysical problems—are like that.

C. S. Lewis[2]

Anyone who has lived for very long can tell you that there are certain questions you will ask that will go unanswered. Following God's path does not leave us immune to facing tragedy or the brokenness of our world. It is not a magic pill that anaesthetizes us from pain and worry. Situations will arise, moments of grief and despair so dire that we are left stunned and unable to cope. There are questions about what we are going through that leave us struggling and grasping for any kind of hope to hold on to. They leave us shattered and wary, not knowing where to turn next.

Now when Jesus returned, a crowd welcomed him, for they were all expecting him. Then a man named Jairus, a synagogue leader, came and fell at Jesus' feet, pleading with him to come to his house because his only daughter, a girl of about twelve, was dying.

Luke 8:40-42 NIV

Jairus and Jesus

Jairus was in one of those dire situations, laced with lethal, hope-killing questions. He was a religious man dedicated to the pursuit of God. But life had dealt his family a cruel blow. His daughter was dying. Time was running out. You can imagine his fear as he pushed through the pressing crowd. What were the questions that were piercing his thoughts, crowding out hope, and leaving him open to despair?

Is my daughter going to make it?
Why is God allowing this?
What have I done to deserve this?

Hole-y Hope

These fear-based questions can pierce through our fragile hope. They leave us with whistling gaps in our faith. Each unanswerable question seems to make the next step forward impossible. How can we keep going when it seems like all is lost? How can we continue when all that we have ever hoped for and believed in is crashing down around our ears? Just like Kate Shelley, we can find ourselves on our knees grappling with circumstances we never asked for and walking out a journey that we don't feel prepared for.

Our journey toward hope can feel very much like crawling across a long treacherous bridge on a stormy night, with the wind threatening to topple us to the plunging depths of despair. We want to stay the course. But we get trapped in the *how, what, why,* and *when* questions of life.

How can I get out of this situation?
What is happening?
Why is God doing this to me?

These are all valid questions. But Jairus chose a different way of looking at things in his time of despair. He shored up his faith and built up his hope with questions of a different nature. His questions changed the course of history for him and everyone around him. Instead of wondering how, what, why, or when, he began to wonder *Who*?

Without Christ, there is no hope.

Charles Spurgeon

Who can help me?
Who can save my daughter?
Who is the healer?

Jairus didn't know why his daughter was dying. He didn't know how long she would be sick. He didn't know if it was too late to go for help. But he was going to find the One person who could help his daughter: Jesus. As a synagogue leader, Jesus might have been a questionable choice. As a grieving father? Jesus was the only choice. News of Jesus' miracles preceded Him. The burgeoning crowds and multiple followers spoke volumes. This was a man you could turn to in a crisis. When all else failed, Jesus didn't. Jairus was on a mission. It was now or never. Jesus was his only hope.

How, what, when, why, or who?

CHAPTER 5

The Who Question

To lovers of the truth, nothing can be put before God and hope in Him.

Saint Basil

Who Is God?

When we start asking the *who* question about who can save us, our faith adventure begins to ramp up. *Who is this God that we are putting all of our hope in?* Our perceptions about His character tend to shape our interactions with Him. They shaped mine. I am a pastor's kid. You would think that I know a lot about God.

I grew up crawling in between the pews of the church. I have hymns and choruses flowing through my veins. I have known the siren song of communion crackers and tiny cups of grape juice for as long as I can remember. I have a very early memory of sneaking out of Sunday school, running down a wide hall, and bursting through the doors of the sanctuary. I couldn't have cared less about the hundreds of people who were listening to my dad speak that morning. I made a beeline for the platform. As I bounded up the steps, my dad didn't miss a beat. He leaned down, picked me up, and held me in his arms. The view from Dad's arms was great. There were lots of smiles and laughter on the faces of the congregants. It was way better than Sunday school.

Sunday school was a bit of a torment for me. First of all, we had to sit still. Stillness was not in my vernacular. We had to memorize verses I didn't understand. Then we listened to Bible stories. They were brutal. Blood and death and gore. They ladled out a healthy helping of judgment. The people who went up against God and Israelites didn't fare well. I always hoped that if I had been born during Bible times, I would have been an Israelite. I wanted to be on God's good side. But I wasn't sure that I would have been.

I wasn't sure because I got in trouble regularly. My mom called me a *curious* child. By this she meant *naughty* child. I had struggles. Even when

I was small, I wanted what I wanted when I wanted it. Sin was a slippery slope that I slid down regularly. Coveting? Stealing? Lying? Punching? Yes, yes, yes, and yes. I once scraped my sister's face with a Mickey Mouse nightlight when she wouldn't give it to me. She still has the scar today. There were moments when my parents despaired of me.

One Sunday night, during a communion service, my mom had to take me out several times for being unruly. With the whisper of prayers and piano playing softly in the background, my mom picked me up and headed out the back door of the sanctuary. She said I called out into the stillness of that moment, "Oh, no! Not again!" I wanted to be good. I really did. But I had no doubt that if God saw what I was up to, in church and out of church, I would be delivered the divine smackdown. In all truth, I was more than a little scared of Him. I was terrified. I thought He was out to get me.

The fear of the LORD is the beginning of wisdom;
all who follow his precepts have good understanding.
To him belongs eternal praise.

Psalm 111:10 NIV

Being Afraid of God

As I have grown both in age and in my understanding of God a bit more, I have realized I had it all wrong. Yes, God is a God of righteousness and justice. He doesn't want us selfishly trapped in sin. There is no doubt about that. But He is so much more than that. He is quite literally so much more than that that we cannot to begin to grasp it. He is glorious. Holy. All mighty. All knowing. All present. How can we even begin to comprehend His greatness?

When people in the Bible came in contact with Him, wrapped in glory, shining like the sun, they passed out. They could not speak. They were paralyzed. They were blinded by His holiness. His greatness. His power. His majesty. He hasn't changed. He was and is too big for us to comprehend. We may try to make Him small so that we can understand Him, but He doesn't try to fit Himself into our understanding or pander to our limitations. He doesn't do small and petty. He does grandiose and awesome. He doesn't do halfway. He does all the way and then some. We will never grasp the amazingness of who He is in His entirety. Not in this lifetime anyway.

But the part of His immense character that He goes out of His way to help us understand is His unfathomable love for us. All that He has done in the past, all that He is doing right now, and all that He will do in the future is born out of a great love for us. That has never changed. With the Israelites, He was constantly reaching out in His love, asking for their repentance, their hearts, and their trust because He wanted to be in relationship with them. He wanted them to have faith in Him. And now, He wants to be in relationship with us. He wants us to have faith in Him. He is not out to squash us with the divine smackdown or crush us with judgment or hold us captive with condemnation. He is not out to get us.

He is out to love us.

He keeps engaging us. He is reaching out to us every single day. He wants in on the details of our lives. He wants to lead us on a journey of hope. God sees our imperfections and loves us anyway. He is not blind. He knows we are scared and broken. So why does He want in on our lives? What is His motivation? Why does He give us so many chances to connect with Him? It is simple really. He is our Dad.

The Thing About Dads

My dad, Dick Foth, is a well-liked and well-respected man. He was a missionary kid, a pastor's kid, a pioneer pastor, and a college president.

He is a world-renowned speaker who has been asked to speak at churches and conferences across the globe. He has been a part of ecumenical discussions at the Vatican. He has opened the United States Senate in prayer. He has had the privilege of knowing great men and doing great things. He is a gifted communicator and a phenomenal storyteller. I have had many, many people throughout the course of my life come up to me and say, "I just love your dad. He is my favorite speaker. It must be great to have him be your dad." I always smile and say, "Yes, it is great to have him be my dad." And it is. But not because he is a great speaker or a good storyteller. When I am with my dad, I don't think of all of his various skill sets. I am just thinking, "This is my dad."

As a tiny girl, when I burst through the doors of the sanctuary and ran up onto the platform into my Dad's arms, I was not thinking, "Man, he is doing a great job with his homiletics this morning." No. I was thinking, "That is my dad. I love him. I want to be with him." He loved me, and I knew it. I have known it since I was a small child. I have grown in it and flourished in it. And it has shaped the person I have become.

For this reason I kneel before the Father, from whom every family in heaven and on earth derives its name. I pray that out of his glorious riches he may strengthen you with power through his Spirit in your inner being, so that Christ may dwell in your hearts through faith. And I pray that you, being rooted and established in love, may have power, together with all the Lord's holy people, to grasp how wide and long and high and deep is the love of Christ, and to know this love that surpasses knowledge—that you may be filled to the measure of all the fullness of God.

Ephesians 3:14-19 NIV

This Great Love

God, our Heavenly Father, wants us to rest in the knowledge that He loves us completely. He wants it to shape how we see Him and how we live out our lives. There is nothing that He would not do for us kids. When sin separated us from Him, He couldn't stand it. He had to make a way for us to burst through the doors of life and leap up into His arms. He did that with His son, Jesus. Jesus put on skin and came to earth in the ultimate turnabout. God became man. No longer was He the God who paralyzed mankind with fear and stunned us with His glorious presence. He was the God who clothed Himself in humanity, who lived and breathed and walked this earth. He was holy, but He was approachable. He was glorious, but He was humble. Jesus was perfect, but He laughed and cried and loved being around little kids and ate fish for dinner. He was one of us.

Jesus lived out all the joys and sufferings on this earth that we live out. And when He took the sins of the world upon Himself and was nailed to a cross, suffering for us, dying for us, He did it with a purpose. He did it so that we could be a part of His family. When Jesus rose on Easter morning, conquering death and shattering the gates of hell, He threw open the doors of heaven and said, "Run on in there. Now you get to know my Dad." A love this great cannot be grasped. But that is Paul's prayer for the Ephesians and God's hope for us. It is only when we realize how much our Heavenly Father loves us that we can begin to place all of our hope in Him. It is only when we recognize that He has held nothing back from us that we hold nothing back from Him.

Love:

Affection. Devotion. Appreciation. Respect. Tenderness.

God is not against us. He never has been. He has always been the God who longs to connect with His kids. He wants to move on our behalf. He wants us to come to Him in every impossible situation. When we ask the *who* question, He is the one and only answer.

Our perceptions and circumstances have shaped the way that we see God. Maybe you have been scared of God and His judgment all of your life. Maybe you feel like He passed you by when He was handing out happiness and joy. Maybe you have never known your own earthly father and cannot even begin to fathom what having a Heavenly Father would feel like. Maybe you are crushed by life's circumstances and can't imagine that there is a way out of the mess you are in. But your journey of hope begins when you understand that your hopes are rooted and established in the love of your Heavenly Father. They are founded in His character. His passion. His purpose. In the darkest part of your journey, your Heavenly Father will not abandon you. He is still at work. He is still on the move. He is surrounding you with love. He is ready to surprise you with hope.

While Jesus was still speaking, someone came from the house of Jairus, the synagogue leader. "Your daughter is dead," he said. "Don't bother the teacher anymore."
Hearing this, Jesus said to Jairus, "Don't be afraid; just believe, and she will be healed."

Luke 8:49-50 NIV

The Face of Hope

With sweat trickling into the edges of Jairus's beard, his forehead touched the dust of the ground. His arms stretched in front of him clutching

Jesus' feet. It felt like someone had just kicked him the stomach. The heat of the day was unbearable. All sense of hope had been ripped from him. Tears dripped off the end of his nose. *Could it be true? Was his daughter dead? Had this race to find the Healer been for nothing?* A wide chasm of fear and despair threatened to open up and swallow him. He felt someone reach down and grip his elbows, pulling him to his feet.

Head up, he looked into the eyes of the Master. The crowd pressed up against his back to hear what Jesus would say. Jairus fought back his tears as he stared into the eyes of the One in whom all of his hopes resided. If Jesus couldn't do something, no one could. Jesus' eyes were kind. His voice was steady. His grip was firm. With a breath of peace and an invitation to faith, Jesus said, "Don't be afraid. Just believe. She will be healed." Jairus was embarking on a faith adventure. The crowd waited to see what he would do. He nodded. Yes. With a smile, Jesus turned and led the way to Jairus's house. It was about to get good. And so the journey of hope begins.

Don't be afraid. Just believe.

CHAPTER 6

The Song of Hope

Every heart sings a song, incomplete. Until another heart whispers back.

Plato

A Mother's Song

Nap time, when I was a child, was a special time. The sun filtered through the golden curtains in our living room home in Urbana. It was warm and quiet. And I nestled up against my mom. She rocked me with a song caught in her throat. I could place a small hand on her neck and feel the song thrumming away. It was a wordless tune. Unless the words in her mind went something like this, "Dear God in heaven, please let Susanna fall asleep. PLEASE." It would have been a good song for her to sing. I wasn't a fan of naps. Naps meant missing out on fun. But I was a fan of fitting into that place where I molded my small body to my mom's, felt her arms around me, and felt the song that she was singing over me. I could have stayed in that place all day long. If I could figure out a way to fit on my mom's lap now, I might give it a go. To go back to that place of peace and comfort would be magical. It was a place where I felt completely attended to in every way.

When my mom thought I was asleep, she would gently get up from the chair, cradling me in her arms, to carry me to my bed. And I would open my eyes and look around. And my mom, bless her heart, would sigh and carry me back to the rocking chair and have one more try at putting me to sleep. And again, I would feel the song she was humming as I rested my head under her clavicle, feeling the steady beat of her heart. It was the song that covered me over and under. That nap-time song wove together the tiny places of my heart with the knowledge that I was wanted and I was loved.

When I got older and I no longer fit on my mom's lap, I would still find her humming. I would lean up over the front of the seat of our station wagon when Dad was driving. Mom sat in the passenger's side directly in front of me. Even though I couldn't hear a thing, I knew she was humming. I knew because her foot was tapping against the plastic floor mat. I would put a gentle hand under her chin and feel the vibration of her vocal chords. "Mom, what song are you singing?" "Just a song." It was a secret melody that had worked its way into her soul. *But what were the words?*

As a mom now, I know the wordless anthem that moms the world over sing for their children. I knew it the moment the nurse laid my first baby on my chest. I memorized it when I felt the tiny thump of my baby's heart against mine. It was a declaration of complete and utter love. I would give up everything to protect him. I wanted every good thing in this world and beyond for him. I would go to the moon and back to ensure that my baby had the best possible life. The depth of what I felt for him was unrivalled. It still is.

Song:
Anthem. Ballad. Hymn. Tune. Melody.

Our Father's Song

In every mother's song is the echo of the song that our Heavenly Father sings over us. Over you. Over me. It is a declaration of love. *What would He give up to take care of you?* Everything. *How many good things does He want for you?* Every good thing. *What lengths would He go to ensure that you have the best possible life?* To the moon and back. In fact, He created the entire universe with you in mind. He knew you before the beginning of time. He knit you together in your mother's womb. He knows you inside and out. He is with you even now. He finds the utmost delight in you. He is chasing you with His love, not rebuking you. He is rejoicing over you with singing.

For the LORD your God is living among you.
He is a mighty savior.
He will take delight in you with gladness.
With his love, he will calm all your fears.
He will rejoice over you with joyful songs.

Zephaniah 3:17

There are times in our life when we know God is near. We feel Him and see Him at work in our lives. It is the place we always long to be. But there are times when He feels far away. We can't see Him. We definitely can't hear Him singing over us. And that is a lonely place to be. Maybe you are too wrapped in fear to hear it. Maybe you have lost sight of Him in the chaos of life. And in losing sight of Him, you have lost sight of yourself. Maybe life has been so disappointing and you are so angry that all you can hear is your own voice shouting into the wind. Or maybe you used to know the feeling of His love and His arms around you, but you have baby-stepped away from your Heavenly Father and don't know how to find your way back. Whatever the reason you feel far away from Him, you are wondering if you have missed your chance. You are wondering if He loves you anymore, if you are forgotten, or if He has stopped singing over you altogether. King David had a couple of thoughts about that.

A Song of Deliverance

King David was known as a man after God's own heart. And at his core, he was a musician. Whether he was in the fields behind his father's house watching over the family sheep herd or in the temple courts with a lyre in his hands, there was a song on his lips. A tune in his heart. A message of praise to be sung. Somehow he had tapped into the song that his Creator was singing over him. That deep song of abiding love. In the face of battle, in the dark depths of the cave, in the glory of victory, there were songs to be written. David chronicled his life's journey with poems and psalms—songs of joy and songs of despair. In every way, he was connected to his Heavenly Father.

Right up until the moment that he wasn't. Somehow he baby-stepped away from God with small choices and made giant mistakes. Living out his selfish desires, he had an affair with Bathsheba. He tried to cover it up. When that failed, he had her husband, Uriah, killed in battle. When he was confronted by God's own prophet Nathan, David saw who he had become. An adulterer. A liar. A murderer. He realized that he was completely responsible for the mess he had gotten himself in. He should have known better. He was God's man, after all. He was beside himself. He begged God for forgiveness.

There was forgiveness for David, but there were also consequences. His baby with Bathsheba died as the result of his sin. His heart was crushed. But in the act of confession, of asking God to change his heart and repenting, he found a song of hope to cling to. He wrote a song that was both steeped in remorse and heavy with hope. God had not forgotten him. God had forgiven him. God was enfolding him with songs of deliverance.

Therefore let all the faithful pray to you
while you may be found;
surely the rising of the mighty waters
will not reach them.
You are my hiding place;
you will protect me from trouble
and surround me with songs of deliverance.

Psalm 32:6-7 NIV

My Song of Deliverance

Sometimes songs of deliverance are hard to hear. We can't make them out above the sound of our tears. I didn't know much about songs of deliverance my junior year of college, but I found myself in a place similar to David. I had baby-stepped away from God, making dumb choices and big mistakes. It's hard to do while you are going to Bible college, but I managed it. With a couple of disastrous relationships in my pocket, a desperate struggle with an eating disorder, and flunking most of my classes, I had pulled out of college. I moved in with my dear aunt and uncle two hours from home, got a job, and went to therapy. I tried to recognize myself in the brokenness that I had visited upon myself with my choices. I didn't know who I had become.

I tried to figure out how to find my way back into God's good graces. I wanted to backtrack and get back to a place where I felt close to Him. But I couldn't find Him. I couldn't find myself. I would crawl up into the loft bedroom where I was staying and cry because I knew I was responsible for the mess I was in. I couldn't undo it. I was scared that I missed out on my chance for redemption. My fear was real. It stuck in my throat. And welled up in my eyes. And poured out into my journal. I was scared that God didn't have anything for me. Any love. Any hope. I was scared that my lot in life was paying for my sins.

When the new school year rolled around, I wasn't ready to go back. With my parents' blessing, I decided to go to a discipleship training school in Hawaii. It was a tough decision, what with the beach and fruity beverages and all. But I sucked it up, packed my bags, and flew to Hawaii. And it was there that I began to try for the first time to hear God above the clamoring voice of condemnation that ruled my thoughts. I wondered if there was a place for me in the presence of a holy and righteous God.

In those weeks of Bible lectures and kitchen duty, of trekking to the beach and sitting in a hammock with my journal, I kept hearing one message over and over again. *God loved me.* And not just a little. A lot. Every week a new speaker would come to talk to us and would talk about God's love. His deep, unending ocean of love that was accessible to all of us. I just wasn't sure if they were talking to me. Because I was a mess.

But as each speaker told his story of love, it was like a thundering wave pounding the shore of my soul. Breaking me down with understanding. Sucking me out into a vast sea of His forgiveness. Pulling me into the wideness of His unfathomable grace.

God's love was for me.
God loved me.
God forgave me.
The good news was for me.

Wave after wave after wave. And His healing? His peace? His restoration? Yes. He wanted to me to have that, too. Even though I had messed up. Even though I should have known better. Even though I was not who I should be. Even though I still struggled. He. Loved. Me.

One of the speakers shared Zephaniah 3:17. In all my years of Scripture memorization, I had never heard that verse. I was floored because of the unlikeliness of it. God is singing this song to His people after they have failed Him repeatedly. After His metaphorical daughter, Jerusalem, had completely messed up. His nation had betrayed Him. But God's punishment was over. He was sweeping up His people in His arms with love. He was beside Himself with joy. And this speaker said, "I want you to imagine this. When it says in the Scripture that God rejoices over you with singing, it literally means that He picks you up and swings you around singing."

And in that hard metal folding chair at the back of the room, I began to cry. It was a new kind of cry. A cry of hope. Because I could picture it in my mind. I could picture how He was swooping down with His arms of grace and catching me up, laughing, swinging me around, holding me close, and shouting with happiness. He was singing over me.

It was the turning point in my life. God's love came crashing in. And the craziest thing happened. I began to love God back. Not fear Him. Not shudder at the thought of Him seeing me in all my mess. Not worry that He was disappointed and would never be able to look at me without judging me again. I longed to know Him. Really know Him. I wanted to hear what He had to say. I wanted to memorize His words. Because it was personal now.

It was me and my Heavenly Father. I would lie in the cotton hammock tied between two banyan trees, the breeze coming up off of the mountains, and feel embraced by love. Like a child in my mother's arms hearing the lullaby she longs to hear. And I knew the words of my Father's song. He loved me. He was singing it over me. He was wrapping me up in it. He was soothing the sore places of my heart with it. He was holding me close. I was finding that place of comfort where I could hear the steady beating of His heart, and I didn't want to let go.

There is no fear in love. But perfect love drives out fear, because fear has to do with punishment. The one who fears is not made perfect in love. We love because He first loved us.

1 John 4:18-19 NIV

Hope Sounds Like Love

God is love. He loved David. He loves me. He loves you. That is the good truth of it. God has been singing a song of hope over us since the beginning of time. It is a song of deliverance and healing. In our darkest moments, when we are lost in despair, He is shouting out across the universe that we don't have to be afraid anymore. He is coming. And He is coming, arms wide open, with a song of love on His lips and a tune of forgiveness that washes us whiter than snow.

God is thundering across the heavens with an anthem of grace. It is a song that finds its melody in the unfathomable love of a Father for His children. It is a soft lullaby of peace and a rousing canticle of freedom. It is a shout of joy. A cry of justice. A hallelujah chorus. As it swoops over and around us, it enfolds us in its truth. The words speak of the endless promises He has for us and in the attributes of His matchless character. It is the kind of song you could listen to for all of eternity.

I love you.

CHAPTER 7

The Hope Sing-Along

He that lives in hope danceth without music.

George Herbert

Wannabe Rock Star

When I was fifteen years old, I loved two things: boys and the *Unguarded* cassette tape by Amy Grant. Not necessarily in that order. I mean boys were good and all. But Amy Grant's music? With its edgy "this is good enough to be on the radio" sound? Amazing. She was turning the Christian music scene on its ear. And she was setting young church-raised girls like me free everywhere. Free to dream. Free to hope. Free to perm our hair and peg our pants and still be followers of Jesus. My cousin, Beth, had bought me the tape. It was like owning a piece of the sun. So bright and shiny and full of life. I would play it over and over and over and over. And I memorized every one of its songs in its entirety. I danced to it using a roll of Christmas wrapping paper as my microphone. In my heart, I was Amy Grant.

Then came that epic day that my friend Cori came to pick me up for school. She was sixteen and had her driver's license. It was a regular day. Like any other. Except for the fact that when she stopped for gas that morning, the gas station attendant was giving away two free tickets to the Amy Grant concert that night. Two free tickets *in the second row*! That is about as close to heaven as you can get. It was clear that God loved us. He was pouring out His blessings upon us. A higher shrieking had never been heard than the moment that Cori told me that she was giving me the other ticket. With our parents' permission, we went to the concert.

The concert was unlike any other I had attended. The music pulsed through the coliseum, sending all of us Amy lovers into a frenzy of joy. We jumped and screamed and cheered. She was so close that we could see the dainty beads of sweat glistening on her brow. We were bathed in the glow of the dazzling lights. The only thing more dazzling than the lights were the sequins that covered Amy's white boots. Arms raised in the air, we sang our hearts out. We knew every song. We knew every word and every dip of every note. And we sang like she was depending on us. We hoped that Amy could hear us above the cacophony of cheering. We wanted her to know how much she meant to us. We screeched in high teenage voices, "We love you, Amy!" And we did. It was a glorious night.

There is something magical about knowing the words of a song. When you sing along with a song, you become more than an audience member; you become a participant. You are a part of the joy. When Cori and I were singing, we were included in something greater than ourselves. Mostly a crush of sweaty, teenage enthusiasm. But we were also praising God. Thousands of voices were raised in recognition of who He was, who He is, and who He always shall be. In that moment in time, we were joining an eternal chorus that has been sung down through the centuries. A song sung to the Creator who is orchestrating this life that we are all a part of. A song of recognition and a song of praise. A song that all of creation has joined in.

God speaks to us in bird and song,
in winds that drift the clouds along,
Above the din and toil of wrong,
A melody of love.

Joseph Johnson

Nature's Choir

You may or may not know that all of creation is singing a song to its Creator. In 2011, British astronomers were able to capture the sound of the stars using a NASA telescope.[1] What they found was astonishing. There was a melody being sung in outer space. Each star has an individual song and frequency. Each song tells a different story of the star's size and its history. NASA also revealed that the stars aren't the only ones singing. The earth sings a song called a "chorus," or a song of radio waves generated in the radiation belts that surround it. The stars are singing. The earth is singing. And it doesn't stop there.

Anyone who has been to the ocean only has to listen to the repetitive breaking of the waves to know it is adding the bass section to the universe's melody. The wind whipping through the aspens in Colorado? The roar of the Amazon River? The thunder of arctic glaciers popping and cracking? The downpour of rain hammering the Cook Islands? Singing. And along with our earth's majestic melody comes the voice of every living creature in every corner of the world. A vast animal choir. Bullfrogs? Check. Hippos? Check. Crickets? Of course. All of creation is singing a song, giving rise to the greatest symphony in existence.

When David wrote about the song of the universe, it was beautiful and poetic. It was also literal.

Let the heavens rejoice, let the earth be glad;
let the sea resound, and all that is in it.
Let the fields be jubilant, and everything in them;
let all the trees of the forest sing for joy.

Psalms 96:11-12 NIV

The song of hope that God sings over us is not a solo. It is not God singing to hear Himself sing. It is call and response. There is a part for each of us. Nature has found its voice. Apparently, it never lost it. Those of us who never knew that God was singing over us didn't know we were supposed to sing back. But He longs to hear us. He wants to hear your song. He wants to hear my song. Just like each star in the sky has a different song to sing, so do we. Just like each celestial body has a different story to tell, so do we.

Sing to the LORD a new song;
sing to the LORD, all the earth.
Sing to the LORD, praise his name;
proclaim his salvation day after day.
Declare his glory among the nations,
his marvelous deeds among all peoples.

Psalm 96:1-3 NIV

Lullabies and Love Songs

The other night, my youngest son, Addie, asked me to come pray for him before he went to sleep. And by pray for him, he meant come lie in bed next to him, with the fan blowing on our faces, talk about the day, and then pray for each other. I went and climbed in next to him. His ten-year-old body is taking up a lot more space than it used to. He put his arm under my neck so he could hold me close, and then he said, "Mom, will you sing me a lullaby?" I used to rock my boys to sleep every night and sing to them. It is rare that they ask for a bedtime song now. I will take it when I can get it. I began to sing some of the songs I used to sing when he was small.

Addie was quiet. Then he said, "Mom, can you sing the Winnie-the-Pooh song?" It's not so much that he likes my voice. He tries to keep me singing as long as possible. He knows as long as I am singing, he doesn't have to go to sleep. The "House at Pooh Corner" lullaby was an old bedtime favorite. I began to sing it. I got through the first verse and chorus, and then I stopped. "Addie, I can't remember the words." This happens more than I would like to admit. He turned to face me, grinned, and picked up where I left off, singing the song to the end. I snuggled him as he sang and joined him on the chorus. He had heard the song so many times it was ingrained in him. "Mom, Dad used to play that song for us every night before we went to sleep. I like that song." "Me, too." What I really liked was Addie singing it. I liked the sound of his voice. The feel of his arm around my neck. The closeness of him. And the song reminded both of us when he was much smaller, a time when we felt close, and all of those snuggly good feelings surrounded us in that moment.

I didn't know how to worship until I knew how to love.

Henry Ward Beecher

The Harmony Line

We are singing a duet with the Creator. Him and us. Singing our hearts out together. We are singing about our Dad. The One who made us and keeps us in the palm of His hand. Our song has a whole lot of verses. Like children singing their Dad's endless praises, we sing across the cosmos. Our Dad is big and strong and amazing and good. And did we mention He is big? Our song is layered with truth about what He has done for us. We all sing our songs differently, but they are variations on a single theme.

Hope.

Each song that we sing is a star bringing its joy and brightness to all who surround us. Telling the story that the Creator is good. Like shimmering globes on a summer string of lights, our songs are added to this world's dark night. Reflecting His glory. Sharing our stories. Telling the world about this Dad who loves us so much. And a funny thing begins to happen when we start singing. The more songs we hear, the more truths we hear about who He is, the more our hope grows. The more we can risk. The more we can dream. The less we are afraid. Story upon story. Hope upon hope. Song upon song.

Creation's song is being sung. It's up to you to decide if you are joining in. No one else can sing your song for you. No one else can share your story of who God is and how He loves you. No one else can tell how He is at work in your life. You have to open your mouth and let it out. Like a crazy teenager at a concert. Or a snuggly ten-year-old at bedtime. Your song is unique and needs to be heard. Even when it's dark. Even when you don't know what is going on. Sing it out anyway.

Faith is the adventure.
Hope is the song.
And your story is the harmony line.

The Creator is singing a song of love and light over you even now. Hope is a duet. What are you singing back?

I am singing over you. Sing with Me.

CHAPTER 8

The Jail Breaker

Hope is the word which God has written on the brow of every man.

Victor Hugo

The Missionary Game

When Scott and I got married, he had been a youth pastor for almost seven years. Being a youth pastor's wife was a new adventure. There was a much higher level of involvement in ministry than I had ever experienced. And it was a different kind of service. The first summer retreat I attended was a baptism by fire. I was not only on the kitchen crew and a camp counselor for one of the girls cabins but also had to play games. Yes, games. And not just any games. Night games. One of our favorite night games that we played was called Missionary. We played holy games, not your run-of-the-mill dodgeball. The other youth pastor's wife, Shelly, and I, along with some of the other adult leaders, hid in the woods surrounding the cabins. Yes, you read that correctly. Our job was to hide out in the dark woods full of critters. At least, full of squirrels. The role we were playing was the underground church. We were desperate for Bibles. The remaining adult leaders were secret police.

The youth group was divided into teams of missionaries. The missionaries were each handed a tiny paper Bible, each team with a different color Bible. The teams' mission was to get their Bible to one of us hidden in the woods without getting caught by the secret police. If a missionary delivered his Bible safely, he crept back to base for the next Bible. If he was caught, he would be put in jail. A missionary could only get out of jail if another missionary came to rescue him and could make it back to home base without being caught again. The team with the most Bibles delivered by the end of the night was the winner.

The game required forest savvy. It was high-stakes play. Youth members brought camo and face paint with them. As youth leaders, we prayed silent prayers as we hunkered down in a patch of ferns, that there was no poison oak hidden among the leaves. Once the missionaries found us, they would spread word of our location to the rest of their team. The secret police were vigilant. If we, as underground church members, were spotted by the secret police, they would use us to lure the missionaries to their demise. They would camp out while waiting for missionaries to arrive and swoop down and haul them off to prison. We had to constantly change our position under cover of darkness. This was confusing to the missionaries who would deliver a Bible to us at one location and come back only to find that we had fled to another spot.

The first time I played Missionary, my heart was beating so loudly it seemed that my body actually believed that the secret police were *real.* I was breathing heavy. I was sweaty. And I had to go to the bathroom. Clearly, I do not fare well in stressful situations. Not even fake stressful situations. This game was played out with stealth and utter quiet. The only sounds to be heard were the crunching feet of the secret police and the shouts of captured missionaries as they were hauled away to prison.

The best part of the game was hearing the patter of feet running toward the prison. Twigs were snapping. There were muffled cries and whispers as they ran past us. The fastest, bravest missionaries were on a mission to break out their compadres. They were risking it all for freedom. The underground church silently cheered them on. We wanted them all free. Then it would happen. Screeches of joy and running feet pounding down the hillside. They made it to the prison, set the captured free, and were running for their missionary lives. The secret police swarmed down the hill after them. The wildness only subsided when the missionaries were back down in the camp, safe at base. Then you heard the rejoicing. Cheering. Laughing. Getting free was invigorating. Freedom always is.

Freedom:
Liberty. Opportunity. Privilege. Unrestraint. Free reign.

The Rock

This past year our family visited Alcatraz for the first time. We took the tour boat out to the small island in the middle of the San Francisco Bay. Surrounded by beautiful gardens and a bird sanctuary, it was picturesque. Waves crashed up on the rocky shore. A crazy dichotomy, really, because no one chose to come to this island of their own accord. The hundreds of inmates who made their home there never got to enjoy the beauty that surrounded it. It was heavily fortified with guards and had state-of-the-art security. Their every move was monitored, from taking showers to eating lunch. The walls were reinforced cement. The cells were so small that you could touch both walls with your arms outstretched. They spent their days trying to find something, anything, to fill the hours. It was a hopeless place to be and a horrible way to live. It was dank and dark inside, despite the fact that the outside of the prison was surrounded by so much loveliness.

The cells nearest to the outer walls were the most coveted by the prisoners because the sun made its way inside the high windows, lighting the corridors. The morning light rarely reached the interior of the prison. But those outer cells were also a kind of torment. Every once in a while, sounds of freedom would seep in through those same windows that lined the walls. The tour recording said many of the inmates recalled the sounds of New Year's Eve. The joy of the city welcoming the incoming year could be heard out across the water. The sounds of the members of the San Francisco yacht club celebrating as they sailed around Alcatraz trickled in and made it into the tiny cells. It was enough to make hardened criminals weep with longing. There was nothing to celebrate as far as they were concerned. Freedom surrounded them on all sides. But no one was coming to set them free.

Cry Freedom

What is it about freedom? Why is it so beautiful? What is it in the breast of every human that longs to be free? It is the echo of the One who created us. The Jail Breaker. The One whose mission is to set us free. It is the song God sang over Joseph as he sat in his prison cell and waited for his dreams to come to pass. The song He sang over the Israelites as they tramped through the wet sand of the Red Sea toward the Promised Land. The song that He sang out in the heat and light of the fiery furnace with Shadrach, Meshach, and Abednego. This is the song of freedom that He has sung over His people time and time again as He came for them. Unlocking doors. Throwing off chains. Breathing new life into them. He is singing that same song over you. You are His people. And He wants you to be free.

The spirit of the Sovereign Lord is on me,
because the Lord has anointed me
to proclaim good news to the poor.
He has sent me to bind up the brokenhearted,
to proclaim freedom for the captives
and release from darkness the prisoners.

Isaiah 61:1 NIV

We have hope because there is no jail cell strong enough to hold Him back. There is no barrier too wide that He cannot breach. There is no captor too strong that He cannot overcome. Maybe you are trapped in self-centered living, feeling the darkness closing in around you. Maybe addiction is written on the door of your cell, and you don't have any idea how to get free. Maybe you are beating your head against the wall, sinking in depression, and sitting down in fear. Now is not the time to let despair creep in. Don't get stuck in the mire of dark thoughts and the lies that the enemy wants you to believe. You weren't designed for desperation and pain. You weren't meant for prison life. You were meant for a life of freedom. Don't give up. Listen. Listen with all of your heart. He is coming in all His glory. Running on fast feet with a song of freedom ringing out in the pitch black night.

I am setting you free.

CHAPTER 9

The Redeemer

I am not what I ought to be. I am not what I want to be.
I am not what I hope to be in another world;
but still I am not what I used to be, and by the grace of God,
I am what I am.

John Newton

Capture the Flag

I have always been competitive when it comes to sports, which is sad because I am not good at sports. During the tryouts for Junior Olympics in fifth grade, my PE teacher, a tall skinny man with thick glasses, looked at me after I completed a sprint. He said, "Did you understand what I said when I asked you to run in a straight line?" His sarcasm was not lost on me. Apparently, I had a little zigzag to my running style. Needless to say, I didn't make the team. But I always put out a great effort. It didn't matter what the sport was. I wanted to win. Dodgeball? Four square? Soccer? You could count on me to run, throw, and kick my hardest even when I had a position I didn't like to play, such as being the jailer during capture the flag. I like to think I was given the job because of my keen awareness and commitment to my work and not because I didn't know how to run in a straight line.

As jailer, I paced back and forth in front of the back stop on the Vine Hill Elementary baseball field. My job was crucial. The kids that sat in my jail waiting for their team were toast. Their eyes scanned the field looking to see if anyone was coming to save them. But I had eyes on them. There was no way they would get free. Until it happened. My PE teacher yelled out in a booming voice, "Jailbreak!" lassoing his arms wildly in the air. That meant prisoners from both teams could leave their jails and make a run for it. If they crossed the midline and made it back to their side of the field without being tagged, they were safe.

I panicked. My prisoners bolted. I didn't know who to go after. I yelled, "Hey!" I tried to give chase, but my light blue Nikes weren't fast enough. Those kids left me in the dust. Freedom was within their sights. My teammates scrambled to catch them before they crossed over to their side of the field. My jail was empty. It hurt my pride a little. And I was more than a little ticked off at my PE teacher. Here I had done all this hard work of guarding, and he was treating the jailbreak like a celebration. Thank goodness recess and snack time were just around the corner. Being a jailer wasn't easy work.

About midnight Paul and Silas were praying and singing hymns to God, and the other prisoners were listening to them. Suddenly there was such a violent earthquake that the foundations of the prison were shaken. At once all the prison doors flew open, and everyone's chains came loose. The jailer woke up, and when he saw the prison doors open, he drew his sword and was about to kill himself because he thought the prisoners had escaped.

Acts 16:25-27 NIV

The Jailer's Story

Unfortunately, there was no recess and snack to look forward to for the jailer in Thyatira, just a rude awakening to a jailbreak crisis. Roused from a deep sleep, the jailer was thrown into confusion as the ground shook beneath him. The roar of the quake brought on the sounds of shifting metal and stone. He pressed himself against the wall, willing the gods to make it stop. The jolting sound of the rumbling earthquake subsided, leaving him trembling and angry. Where were the guards? Were they keeping watch over the prisoners? As the dust settled, the jail keeper stepped out into the corridor. He squinted, letting his eyes adjust to the darkness. He looked down the row of prison doors. Every single door was thrown open. Every door.

He felt a sick sensation in the pit of his stomach. Not one of his prisoners would remain. There was no way he could keep them from escaping now, especially the new prisoners that he had received special instruction to keep under lock and key: Paul and Silas. They were strange prisoners. They had been beaten severely, but their songs of praise in the night were what had lulled him into his deep sleep. His hands began to shake. His honor was at stake. He fumbled for his sword. He knelt before it, knowing what he had to do. He would lean into the blade, meeting his fate. Life for him was over.

And then from the dark corner of a cell came a shout, "Don't harm yourself! We are all here!" He jumped up and the sword fell, clattering to the floor. With a yell, he called to the guards, "Bring the lights!" Could it even be true? Could the prisoners all be accounted for?

The jailer called for the lights, rushed in and fell trembling before Paul and Silas. He then brought them out and asked, "Sirs, what must I do to be saved?" They replied, "Believe in the Lord Jesus, and you will be saved—you and your household." Then they spoke the word of the Lord to him and to all the others in his house. At that hour of the night the jailer took them and washed their wounds; then immediately he and all his household were baptized. The jailer brought them into his house and set a meal before them; he was filled with joy because he had come to believe in God—he and his whole household.

Acts 16:29-34 NIV

Condemnation and Judgment

When the jail keeper went into work that day, he had no idea that he was the one who was actually in prison. He didn't know that he was far from Christ. He didn't recognize that he was lost in sin and would die not knowing his Creator. As he ordered Paul and Silas to be put in chains with extra guards surrounding them, he was doing what he was paid to do. The jailer thought he was in control. What he wasn't counting on was the God of the Universe shouting, "Jailbreak!" And when the shout came, God wasn't just offering freedom for Paul and Silas, who were singing His praises; He was offering freedom for the jailer, too.

We aren't really full of grace toward people when it comes to crimes committed. We are judge-y and harsh. We want freedom for the people who we think deserve freedom. We want the captive to be set free. But the captor? Let's give him what he's got coming to him. It is a good thing that we aren't God. God has loads of grace, and it is based not on our offenses or how good or bad we are. It is based on one thing alone: the redemptive sacrifice of His Son, Jesus.

God's grace covers *all* sin. That has always been His plan from the beginning. The Scriptures say that *all* have sinned and fallen short of the glory of God. And that it is His desire to draw *all* men to Him. *All* is a big word to be contained by three small letters. It is an inclusive, arms-wide-open kind of word. When it comes to *all*, no one is exempt. Not from His vast stores of forgiveness. Or His unfathomable reaches of redeeming love. Grace is for everyone. For you. For me. For Paul. And for the jailer who had Paul under lock and key. Jesus didn't just come to save the captives. He came to save the captor, too.

Redemption and forgiveness go hand in hand. Jesus forgives our sins, our deepest darkness, our greatest shame and then turns around and uses it to bring Him glory. It is the way that He works in the world. In us. He takes all of our pain, our indecency, our dirty secrets, and He clothes us in His righteousness. He covers our shame and, in return, asks us to do the same for those around us.

Paul knew a thing or two about imprisoning Christians. It wasn't long before the midnight jailbreak that he had been called Saul and was delivering the disciples of Jesus up to jail himself. Saul had stood by in self-righteous anger and watched a Christ-follower, Stephen, die, martyred by stoning. And even more, Saul had felt he was right to stone Stephen. He thought Stephen was a blasphemer because Stephen recognized Jesus as the Son of God. It wasn't until Jesus showed up on the road to Damascus, with all of His bright glory and truth, that Saul recognized Jesus for who He was. His Savior. Saul also saw himself for who he was in God's eyes. A betrayer. A persecutor. A murderer. It flattened him.

But Jesus didn't leave him there, shattered. Jesus did the one thing no one else could: He offered Saul a path different than persecutor. He offered him a new name. In that moment, Saul became a new creation. As Paul, facedown in the dust, he yielded his life, body, mind, and spirit to Jesus. And Jesus didn't judge him. He restored Paul with His love. He lavished him with His grace. He built him up with hope by opening the door for Paul to have a new life. Jesus was offering redemption. So it is not a surprise that Paul is the first to offer the Thyatira jailer that same life-changing grace. It is no shock that he was willing to forgive the harsh treatment he received. He had been there, done that. Instead of judging the jailer and making sure he got what he has coming to him, Paul cracks open the door of grace. It is so beautiful to behold that the jailer falls at his feet. He begs Paul to lead the way to this new life. Not just for him but for his entire family. He cannot wait another minute to get in on it.

Condemnation:
Accusation. Judgment. Blame. Reproach. Doom.

What does it mean to be redeemed? What does it mean to live a life flooded with grace? Not only is there freedom from sin. From darkness. From weakness. From our own selfish way of living. But it also means that our offenses are not held against us. Jesus' sacrifice is our get-out-of-jail-free card. He served our time so that we wouldn't have to. He has paid the penalty for our sins. He has come to free us with His love. He is not condemning us. He is giving us a new way of living and thinking. A mind-set that is steeped in hope, not shame. He wants us to step into the grace-filled life He has for us. When you experience God's song of redemption being sung over your life, you experience a life of amazement. Because you receive a life that you don't deserve.

Therefore, there is now no condemnation for those who are in Christ Jesus, because through Christ Jesus the law of the Spirit who gives life has set you free from the law of sin and death.

Romans 8:1-2 NIV

The Song of the Redeemed

No one knew the power of the grace-filled life better than John Newton, the former slave trader turned pastor. John was licentious, blasphemous, hate filled, lustful, and money hungry. He was known for his harsh treatment of slaves, keeping his ship's guns trained on the slave quarters to quell any uprisings. His slave-trading years were turbulent. He almost lost his life in a storm. He was deserted by his ship and was taken as a slave himself. But eventually, he went back to the trade. His life was full of violence and fear. But God had a different plan for John the persecutor.[1]

There was a steady outpouring of God's love and grace over his life. Not just for a moment but for years. Over the long years, John experienced God's song of redemption. Even after John began to experience God's grace and love, he continued to deal in slavery for several years. Sometimes it takes a lifetime for grace to flood every corner of our hearts. The journey of grace is not perfect; there are many twists and turns. But over the years, John's heart began to change, and his life began to look different. It was a long road from the slave ship to the village vicarage. Even longer from vicar to becoming the mentor of William Wilberforce, the parliament member who brought about the end of the slave trade in England.

When the prime minister called for a special council on slavery, Newton was brought in to testify on behalf of ending slavery. No one knew the ins and outs of the horrors of slavery like he did. No one knew the brutality and the inhumanity of it better than a former slave trader. By grace, John had come full circle, fighting against the very trade that he had promoted. God used John's greatest sin to bring about freedom for the next generation. Newton ended his days serving in a church in London. Over the hearth in his vicarage hung a plaque with these words:

> Since thou wast precious in my sight thou hast been honourable: but thou shalt remember that thou wast a bond-man in the land of Egypt, and the Lord thy God redeemed thee.[2]

The song of the redeemed is a powerful song.

Amazing grace, how sweet the Sound,
That saved a wretch like me.
I once was lost. But now I'm found.
Was blind but now I see.

John Newton

Hope Feels Like Grace

God is in the business of using our worst mistakes for His greatest glory. He can use every wrong choice, every poor decision that buries us in shame, and shape it into our song of redemption. And we, in turn, can sing along and set others free, pulling them along on the path of freedom. God's work in us is not defined by our past. He sings out grace and peace over us, covering our sins and offering us a new way to live.

Hope is a song of grace, grace, and more grace. It is a jailbreak song full of second chances and new life. It is the song that God is singing over you now. He sees your heart. He knows your past. He holds your life in His hands. And He sings, "Redeemed."

I am redeeming you.

CHAPTER 10

The Storm Whisperer

In the presence of the storm, thunderbolts, hurricane, rain, darkness and the lions, which might be concealed but a few paces away, he felt disarmed and helpless.

Henryk Sienkiewicz

Surviving a Tigernado

I am not a wilderness person. The closest I like to get to the woods is watching *National Geographic* documentaries. I like to look at nature; I just don't want to be in nature. My friends who love to camp don't understand this. What could be more alluring than a night in the outdoors? What could be more relaxing than fresh air and the deep piney scent of a mountain breeze? I don't know. Maybe the scent of suntan lotion and a heavily chlorinated hotel pool? That sounds pretty relaxing to me. And there are usually fewer bugs and fewer chances of getting struck by lightning at a hotel. It's not that I don't enjoy nature's beauty. It's that I am intimidated by its wildness, the fact that around any corner could be a wild animal or a flash flood. That is the thing about nature. It's so unpredictable.

Last spring, I flew into Oklahoma City for a speaking engagement at my friend, Rene's, church. It was a bit of bumpy landing due to the storm coming in. When I got off of the escalator at the baggage claim, Rene was waiting for me. I said, "Rene! You are so nice! I can't believe you came in to meet me." Rene hugged me and then said, "Well, Sue, we have a tornado coming." To which I said, "What? Right now?" She tried to look upbeat, "Yep. Right now. But don't worry. These things happen all the time. So we were staying put at the airport in case we needed to take shelter." Taking shelter is not something we do in California, what with the constant sunshine and all. But I was quick to learn that not only was a tornado headed our way but also flash floods and hail were imminent. Nature was doing its thing, and it was a three-for-one.

As the storm closed in, the tornado sirens started going off. It's a kiss-your-mama-good-bye kind of sound. We were evacuated into the tunnels below the airport with about five hundred other people. Rene was talking me through the drill. Usually you are down in the tunnels for about thirty minutes until the storm passes. As she tracked the storm on her phone radar like a seasoned meteorologist, I sent frantic texts to my family for prayer. I was basing my level of fear by the look on Rene's face. If she wasn't freaking out, I would try not to freak out. I told her this: "If you're not scared, then I won't be scared." I lied. I was totally scared. But she proceeded to keep a look of absolute serenity on her face throughout the eight-hour ordeal.

Yep. Eight hours. Even when we got evacuated for a second time down in the tunnels. Even when I was lying flat on the ground, trying to use the cold floor tiles to ice my ever-tensing back muscles. Even when there was a tornado sighted on the runway. Even when the storm decided to sit on top of the airport and linger for the evening. The only time Rene almost lost her cool was when we came up from the tunnels between tornadoes and the guy at the coffee kiosk wouldn't sell us any coffee or muffins. You should never withhold muffins from people who haven't eaten in eight hours. Lucky for him, we tracked down a vending machine. It could've gotten ugly.

The tornado passed and was followed by flash flood warnings and hail. Rene took every weather change in stride like it was just another spring day. Like there wasn't the possibility of drowning, being concussed by baseball-sized hail, or being sucked up into the vortex of a tornadic storm at a moment's notice. We just had to wait until the flood waters receded in the streets so we could get home. We went up to her car to recharge our phones and listen to the radio for the all clear. With the sound of tornado sirens going off to the east and the terrifying bleat of the emergency broadcast system echoing through the car, a final emergency warning came over the radio, "Breaking news! A safari park has been hit by a tornado. There are tigers and exotic animals on the loose. Stay inside."

We looked at each other. In what reality do you have tornadoes, hail, flash floods, and *tigers*? At this, Rene's calm began to waver. And then she cracked. "Tigers? You have got to be kidding me!" She started laughing so hard she was almost crying. I had to laugh with her. "Tigers? Exotic animals? I've got nothing." There was no way she could spin this one for me. Nature in all its unpredictability was coming at us.

We must free ourselves of the hope that the sea will ever rest. We must learn to sail in high winds.

Aristotle Onassis

There are a lot of things in life that we think we should be able to control. We work so hard to find a place of security where we feel safe. We want to ensure that life goes the way that we want it to. But so few of us have super powers. Not one of us knows how to control the wind or, say, a large tiger coming at us. It only takes a glimpse of nature in all of its power to undo that feeling of security. A moment in a hailstorm, the view of a rushing tsunami, the rumbling of an earthquake? These things show us how powerless we really are. The wilderness shows us how little we actually control. The disciples discovered this firsthand.

A Moment with Nature

After a day of seeing miraculous healings, one would think that everything would be great. Jesus had healed many with a simple touch. When the centurion came to Him with a request to heal his servant, Jesus healed him from afar. His miraculous strength was stunning. People could not get enough of Him. With crowds pressing in from every side, Jesus and His disciples stepped inside the boat to cross the lake. Water slapped up against the roughened sides as the crowds moved forward. No one wanted Him to leave.

The disciples pushed off of the bank and Jesus, exhausted from a full day of ministry, hunkered down to catch a much-needed nap. The winds began to pick up. The gentle sloshing of lake water quickly became waves breaking over the bow. They weren't even halfway across the lake. Thunder rolled across the blackening sky. Flashes of lightning revealed the mounting fear on the disciples' faces. They had gone from the exhilaration of watching Jesus do countless miracles to the unfettered terror of realizing that they were going to die. And through the entire ordeal, Jesus was sleeping. Napping. How was this even possible? It is possible because Jesus knew something the disciples don't know. He controlled the waves. Plain and simple.

What they didn't realize in their panic was that His connection with nature didn't stop there. He also controlled the wind. He controlled the heavens. He controlled oceans and rivers and tiny creeks. He controlled tornadoes and earthquakes and floods. He did then, and He does now. He can hold back the tide with a breath and dissipate storm clouds with a word. He is the King of Glory. Every force of nature bows to Him without a word. Why? Because He created them. They do His bidding. They come and go at His pleasure. He is not afraid of their forcefulness or power. They are merely an echo of His own.

Then he got into the boat and his disciples followed him. Suddenly a furious storm came up on the lake, so that the waves swept over the boat. But Jesus was sleeping. The disciples went and woke him, saying, "Lord, save us! We're going to drown!" He replied, "You of little faith, why are you so afraid?" Then he got up and rebuked the winds and the waves, and it was completely calm. The men were amazed and asked, "What kind of man is this? Even the winds and the waves obey him!"

Matthew 8:23-27 NIV

George's Story

George was hoping that God was listening when he knelt in his wheat field on the sweeping Ontario prairie. His kids and wife were back in the farmhouse taking shelter. The livestock were already in the barn. They knew what was coming. Blackish-purple clouds gathered in an ominous pattern in the sky. The patter of rain began to fall. Wind whipped through the stalks of wheat and slapped at his face. George wasn't a crying man, but he could feel the knot forming in his throat. He was a pioneer. He had weathered storms before. He had known hardship. He was tough. But he knew that if this coming hailstorm barreled through his crops, all was lost. Not just for him, but for every wheat farmer for miles around. That meant no seed for next year. No money from the crops. It meant hunger for his family and his animals.

George prayed a simple prayer as the wheat swayed like ocean waves. He prayed, "God, I am asking you to save this crop." George got up from his knees. He knew that there was nothing he could do to hold back the storm. But he also knew that the God he believed in controlled the elements. He had heard stories in the Bible about the calming of the waves and the parting of seas. He was betting on the One who placed the stars in orbit and spoke galaxies into existence.

The hailstorm blew over the prairie, flattening every field of wheat for miles. Except for George's. When it came up to his field, it passed to the other side without dropping a piece of hail. The golden shafts of wheat were unbroken, unbent by the storm. It was a miracle. It sounds impossible, but this story has been passed down in my family. It was my great-grandpa's miracle. George Harvey Presnell was able to harvest his field, feed his family, and give seed to all the surrounding farms for the coming year. His answered prayer yielded hope not just for him but for all of us who have come along after him, reminding us that our hopes are in the God who cares about tiny heads of wheat and a farmer's dreams. He holds back winds and hail. God doesn't even have to try. He is that powerful. That mighty. That glorious.

Where does your security lie? Is God your refuge, your hiding place, your stronghold, your shepherd, your counselor, your friend, your redeemer, your savior, your guide? If He is, you don't need any further security.

Elisabeth Elliot

After the waves flattened out like glass and the wind became a whisper, the disciples had to rethink everything. They would never look at Jesus the same way again. Healing a servant was one thing. Calming a gale-force wind with a word? That was something different altogether. This was truly God in their midst, using His power and creativity on their behalf and calming storms. My great-grandpa would never see a wheat field without remembering how God stepped in, in His mercy and provision, and held back a hailstorm from destroying his crop. God met him at the point of his greatest need and offered hope. Hope for him. Hope for every farmer in that region.

Then they cried out to the Lord in their trouble,
and he brought them out of their distress.
He stilled the storm to a whisper;
the waves of the sea were hushed.
They were glad when it grew calm,
and he guided them to their desired haven.

Psalms 107:28-30 NIV

The One who loves us most of all speaks, and the oceans listen. He is the Storm Whisperer. He soothes raging waters. He shuts lions' mouths. He parts seas. All that is in the natural world is under His control. All of creation bends to His will. He brings peace to chaos. Both literally and figuratively. In the spiritual realm and the physical realm. Our hope rides on the One who owns the wind and walks on water. It is bound up in the One who has never been afraid of a storm a moment in His life. And God is singing a song of peace over us. A song of calm and clear waters. A song that brings thunder and lightning to a halt and cracks open a clear blue sky. A song that reminds you that you are secure in His presence, even while the storm rages around you.

I am calming the storm.

CHAPTER 11

The Time Keeper

Hope is patience with the lamp lit.

Tertullian

The Waiting Game

Waiting has never been my strong suit. It could possibly be my greatest weakness. But for anyone who is a writer or who is trying to be a writer, it should be the number one line item in the job description. You are going to be waiting. A lot. There are a lot of emotions involved in waiting. Excitement. Expectancy. Boredom. Despair. I have experienced all of those emotions in the space of one day. Especially when waiting to see if one of my manuscripts has made it through a publishing committee. Will they like it? Will they hate it? Am I going to be offered a contract to write the book? Are they going to pass on it? Will my hopes be dashed? My fate hangs in the balance.

The longest I have ever waited on having a book published is thirteen years. Over a decade. And those thirteen years came after the five years of attending writing conferences and developing the chops to actually write a book. People don't tell you that your dreams can take eighteen years to come true. They don't tell you this because then you would look at them and say, "I think I am going to lie down and die now." Waiting is that hard. It can literally suck the life right out of you.

Waiting feels a lot like rejection. And in most writer's cases, it is actual rejection. People look at your work and say things like, "Yep. I don't like that." Or, "You need a year or seven more to rework this." And you are expected to smile and say, "Thanks so much for your time." When what you really want to say is, "Why are you so mean?" Lashing out in anger is a normal reaction to rejection.

My thirteen-year publishing wait began with my book proposal making it all the way through both the editorial and publishing committees. It was the first time one of my proposals had made it that far. The book was a go. I was thrilled. The next step in the process was for the publishing company to offer me a contract to write the book. I flew down to Los Angeles and spent time with the publisher. He said it was a done deal. Later that week I got a call from him. He said, "We have decided we don't think this book is a good fit for our company. We're so sorry." A giant lump tightened in my throat. I said "thank you" and "good-bye" and sat on my couch and wept. I felt like I was saying "thank you" and "good-bye" to my dream. I had the thought, after all these years of waiting and rejection, that maybe writing wasn't a good fit for my life.

Within that month, I got two more rejection letters. One for a humorous book on pregnancy, about which the responding editor told me that he thought my description of being nauseous was gross and that I was better than that. I wasn't better than that. Being nauseous actually is super gross. And then I got a second letter from a publishing company rejecting a writing sample they had requested so they could see my different styles of writing. It wasn't even a book proposal for publication. I was so angry, I cried. I told Scott, "It is one thing to get rejected for something that I have submitted for publication. It is a completely different story to get rejected for something I didn't even offer them." As Scott held me, I wept into his shoulder. "I am done with writing. It's too hard. It hurts too much."

For the next three years, I focused on being a mom. I had three little ones ages five and under. I was exhausted and wild. But the writing dream? It wouldn't go away. It was in me. I had to get all I was going through down on paper. And I wanted to talk to other people about it: "Are you exhausted and wild, too?" and "How long has it been since you have showered?" and "Jesus keeps showing up in the mess of my life. Is He showing up in yours?" Those questions begged to be answered with all of the big feelings I was feeling. The computer came back out. I began to write my life. Live my dream. Hope against hope that maybe, just maybe, someone would like what I had to say. Ten years after my first writer's conference, my first book came out.

Those who do not hope cannot wait; but if we hope for that we see not, then do we with patience wait for it.

Charles Spurgeon

The Long Dream

Some dreams take decades. The original book that the publisher passed on, thirteen long years ago, came out this year. And I wept again. This time for joy. Because God is so good. And His timing is never off. Even though I could have sworn it was horribly off. Even though I had begged Him to let this dream of mine come true. He knew better. This book is one hundred times better than it would have been thirteen years ago. It carries the weight of experience and hope and love. It has a million more prayers backing it up. It is not the book that I hoped for. It is the dream God launched into existence. At just the right time.

How does He know how things should work out? How does He weave together His great plans? How does He decide what should go where and when to intervene and shape our lives? How does He put up with our weeping and gnashing of teeth when we don't get what we want when we want it?

Do you not know?
Have you not heard?
Has it not been told you from the beginning?
Have you not understood since the earth was founded?
He sits enthroned above the circle of the earth,

and its people are like grasshoppers.
He stretches out the heavens like a canopy,
and spreads them out like a tent to live in.

Isaiah 40:21-22 NIV

His Time, His Timing

God is outside of time. He has no beginning and no end, but He holds our beginning and our end within the span of His hands. This is incredibly difficult for us to comprehend. Everything we know about life is held in the confines of time. How can He possibly be aware of all humanity, each of us with our individual needs at any moment of any day? How can He possibly know about our hopes and dreams? How does He know when to move on our behalf or when to close a door for, say, thirteen years? Probably because He made us. He gave us those dreams. He sees it all. And He knows when to move.

My boys are LEGO fanatics. I appreciate their developmental qualities that inspire creativity. I have less appreciation for them when they are strewn across the floor and waiting for me to impale my heel upon them. I have told my boys several times, "If they are not picked up, they will be vacuumed up." This is a great motivator because every LEGO has a purpose and a place. The boys have built small universes out of them. They have crafted entire villages, worlds, and cosmos out of these mini building blocks. And then they tear them apart and rebuild them. They are forever inspired to keep moving and restructuring. They know exactly where they want each piece, and they are completely aware of each minute block at all times, down to the last tiny detail. They love these small worlds that they craft. My boys are completely invested. They don't want one single block to go missing.

In a tiny way, this mirrors how the Time Keeper views us. He sits above the circle of the earth. We are like grasshoppers in His eyes. And oh, how He loves us with our tiny lives and tiny hearts and tiny minds. We are too small to comprehend His grand plan and the complex world that He has built around us. But He is completely aware of us, our purpose, our joy, and our pain. His feelings about us are not small. His thoughts about us number in the millions, more than the grains of sand. He knows every detail about us, and He delights in those details.

Wait:
Pause. Delay. Halt. Hold up. Stay.

We, in our finite smallness, try to dictate what we think His next move should be. We try to tell Him dates and times that would best fit our comprehension of our lives. But He sees all. Knows all. And is all-powerful. And sometimes He asks us to wait upon Him and His timing. To wait and trust in His impeccable choices. To wait and know that He is the One who laid the very foundation of the earth. And if we can just give Him a second to order points A to Z, the life that He is creating for us is so much more than we could ever dream of.

Isaiah 40:31 (NIV, emphasis added) says,

> *But those who* hope *in the* L*ORD*
> *will renew their strength.*
> *They will soar on wings like eagles;*
> *they will run and not grow weary,*
> *they will walk and not be faint.*

But the King James translation reads, "They that *wait* upon the LORD" (emphasis added). Hope. Wait. Hope. Wait. Hoping and waiting are interchangeable. They seem opposite. "Hope" springs up, full of goodness and light. "Wait" seems to writhe in angst and uncertainty. How are the two even compatible?

> *What then are we to do about our problems? We must learn to live with them until such time as God delivers us from them. . . . We must pray for grace to endure them without murmuring. Problems patiently endured will work for our spiritual perfecting. They harm us only when we resist them or endure them unwillingly.*
>
> *A. W. Tozer*

Sarah's Story

Even though we don't like waiting, our strength comes when we place our hope in the One who has perfect timing. He always comes through for us. Dreams can be years in the making. Sarah was an authority on this. God promised her and Abraham a child. In those long, dusty days of following God, Sarah had longed for a baby to hold in her arms. She watched woman after woman around her give birth. She had cried for so many years that her tears had dried up. When God actually promised Abraham they would have a son, Sarah overheard the conversation and laughed. Not in a good way. But in a "Yeah, right" kind of way. She was so full of pain and sorrow. The bitterness of never holding a sweet-smelling baby of her own in her arms consumed her. Sometimes dreams hurt too much. It is easier to give them up than to bear up under the burden of an unfulfilled dream.

Sarah waited twenty-five years before she held that fulfilled promise in her arms. That was twenty-five years after the decades of normal child-bearing years that she had lived through. That is a long time to hold onto a dream, to hope for the impossible. Sarah didn't always get the hoping right. When she convinced Abraham to sleep with her maid, Hagar, it wasn't her most shining moment. Sometimes we try to fulfill God's promises on our own. We try to manipulate His timing. It rarely ends well. So Sarah kept waiting. She kept alive a small kernel of hope that God was going to do what He said. This didn't mean she wasn't scared or freaked out. This didn't mean she didn't have moments of despair. It means that she kept coming back to the promise that God gave her and Abraham. She kept reaching for His truth. She kept believing He was who He said He was and, when He was ready, would do what He promised.

And in the wait, even when Abraham and Sarah didn't realize it, they exercised their faith muscles. They were doing trust reps and hope lunges. They were running a hope marathon, keeping their eyes focused on the One who loved them most of all. They were strengthening their belief that the God who keeps time in His hands was keeping track of them. Holding their dreams in His palm. They told themselves that they weren't forgotten and that the God who sits above the circle of the earth saw them and knew them.

And when dawn cracked on that day of Isaac's birth, Sarah's yells lit up the camp. Yells of childbirth and expectation. Dreams are almost always hard work. And then the cries of her baby pierced the air. Sarah, sweat pouring down the sides of her face, held that sweet boy to her chest. She gulped in great gasps of air, covered his small perfect forehead with kisses, and began to laugh. Not a "Yeah, right" kind of laugh, but the bubbling kind of laughter that fills the room and invites everyone to join in. The kind of laughter that comes from a soul overtaken by joy. It comes with the recognition that God, in all His might and His power, has done what He promised, and here you are holding that promise in your arms.

What Thou wilt, when Thou wilt, how Thou wilt.

John Newton

Hope = Waiting

If you are waiting on God right now, on the dreams He has placed in your heart, and on the promises that He has spoken out over your life, you are running a marathon of hope. You are exercising and building up your trust muscles. And He is at work. Even if you don't know it. Even if you can't hear Him. Even if you have given up your dream only to pick it back up again. He is renewing your strength. So in the right moment, you will be able to run. Like the wind. And not grow weary. So that you will walk for days upon days upon days and not feel like you are going to die.

God is building up your faith muscles so that in that perfect moment, you can soar on wings like eagles, giving you a bird's-eye view of everything He is accomplishing in your life. Your time frame is not His time frame. He sees all. He knows all. He is able to do anything, and God is singing a song of strength over you. It is a waiting song, full of promise that will come to pass at exactly the right moment, in exactly the right way. He is birthing a dream in you. It will surprise you with joy and show you that the Time Keeper knows you better than you know yourself. And that's a promise.

I am always on time.

CHAPTER 12
The Story Writer

If you want a happy ending, that depends, of course,
on where you stop your story.

Orson Welles

A Plot Twist

The spring after I attended the discipleship training school in Hawaii, overflowing with God's love and grace, I found myself on a missions outreach in Albania. I was there for two months, but it felt like two years. In case you didn't know, Albania is not an island paradise. Albania has a long, storied history. Its beautiful people had been terrorized for centuries. This small nation, perched above Greece, has a past filled with occupation since before the time of Christ. It was a stop-off on one of Paul's missionary journeys. Both the Roman Empire and Ottoman Empire had dominated its borders. This is a place that has dealt with loss and turmoil for hundreds of years. This is not the land of relaxation and white sand beaches. Its people have fought long and hard to survive.[1]

When our team landed at the airport, we entered the country on the heels of the first democratic election. Ever. For forty years, Albania had declared itself an atheist nation. It had been under the Communist thumb, terrorized and bullied by the dictator Enver Hoxha,[2] who had tortured both Christians and Muslims for their faith. It is safe to say that this country was still finding its feet in the democratic process. There was chaos as the government was sorting itself out. Enter me, in my own state of chaos.

Our team was supposed to support a local missionary in establishing a Bible study in one of the outlying villages. We were all staying in homes with Albanian families. We would meet up each day in the city center for prayer and to go out into the surrounding villages. It sounded doable. We would be sharing the love of Jesus and helping the local church. We thought it was going to be exciting. And it was. But not in the way I thought it would be. We were naive to the ways of the world, as we would soon find out.

Being in Albania meant complete immersion in a male-dominated culture. Our team had a lot of tall, fair-haired women. We stood out like a bunch of blonde Amazons in a city of short, dark men. Culture dictated that we had to keep our heads down and not make eye contact with the men. Looking into the eyes of a man was seen as a sexual advance. Despite keeping our heads down, our eyes trained on the ground, and not inviting any types of advances, there was a lot of pinching and whistling going on. This was an affront to all my sensibilities.

I had a lot of trouble being holy and thinking about Jesus when strange men were pinching my rear. I definitely was not thinking about telling them how Jesus loved them and wanted to offer them hope. Mostly, I wanted to punch them. I won't lie. I did punch a few. This is why Scott will not allow me to speak at missions Sundays at our church. He says my stories aren't holy; mostly, he means I am not holy. He is so right.

On top of the culture shock, I was also struggling with weight gain, which shouldn't have been a big deal. But it was a big deal. I had just completed six months of counseling for an eating disorder prior to coming to Albania. The host family we lived with were wildly fond of oil and bread and sometimes fatty meat but not a whole lot of vegetables. This was completely understandable. There were not a lot of food sources available, except on the black market. This was a country in crisis. We ate what we were offered. But there was a lot of offering going on. In Albania, the guests are given the largest portions—and multiple portions—of whatever food is being served.

Our host family sacrificed on our behalf and gave us more than three times the amount of food they would serve themselves. We didn't want to offend them and refuse their amazing hospitality because they were so kind. But my pants were so tight. Really, really tight. Like I-couldn't-breathe-when-I-sat-down tight. And it wasn't like I could go out and buy another pair of pants. Most Albanian women are around 5 feet tall, and I am 5' 8". I would have been buying knickers. I am pretty sure that revealing my calves in public would have caused a riot in the town square.

Everything felt wrong in Albania. I thought missionary life was supposed to be the crowning glory of my discipleship training school. God had been healing me and teaching me so much about His love. I thought this experience would complete me somehow. Instead, I was realizing that being a missionary was being yourself in a place where you were completely out of sorts. All you are doing is uprooting yourself from all you know and taking all your issues with you to another country. You are vulnerable. It wasn't glorious. It was hard.

I had grown up reading missionary stories and of the triumphs of bringing others to Christ. Of miracles. Of lives changed. Somehow I had managed to skip over the parts of these stories during which these missionaries faced fear and doubt. Where they work hard and struggle. But every day in Albania was a struggle for me. And each struggle seemed to lay me bare, revealing my doubts and my sins. I spent my days, head down, trying to deflect groping hands, being angry at not being able to exercise my American rights (these apparently only work in America), and battling the desire to make myself throw up so I could zip up my pants. I wasn't bringing anyone to Christ. I felt like I was losing my salvation. I had been plopped down in the middle of some nightmarish story in which I was having to face all my weaknesses at once.

I was, in fact, living out a story. My story. Complete with complex plot twists and arch nemeses. The story line went something like this. Just imagine a girl on the brink of womanhood who has struggled for years with her self-worth, who repeatedly makes bad relationship choices with boys who did not value her, and who, on top of that, wants to throw up to make herself feel better. Now put her as a missionary in a country full of men who look at her as less than worthy and have her live with a host family who force-feeds her fried bread. Then remind her daily that she can't give in to her eating disorder because she is supposed to be holy now. She is supposed to be shining the Light of hope to all around her. *Supposed to* would be the operative words here.

What will happen? Will she have a nervous breakdown? (Yes.) Will she cry when her pants get too tight? (Yes.) Will she punch strange men in the chest? (Yes.) Will she survive? (Just barely.) Will she ever be free of her eating disorder? (Yes.) Will she realize that her self-worth is not connected to what other people think of her? (Yes.) And the biggest question of all, will she trust God to work out His story for her in spite of it all? If I am honest, that last question is still in play. Because God is still writing my story. Albania was just one chapter in my life. With every chapter that I walk out, I am faced with this question: Will I let Him have His way in me? Will I yield my story line to Him? Will I trust Him to write my life in His terms with His point of view? He is the Master Story Writer. The Author and Perfector of my faith. And yours.

Story:
History. Narrative. Drama. Adventure. Cliff-hanger.

Rewrites and Edits

My friend Rene (of Tigernado fame) is a screenwriter. She has an amazing way of shaping stories and enriching plotlines. In the novels that she has written, she weaves multiple narratives lines together, revealing her characters' strengths and weaknesses. She blends them together into a completely satisfying tale. She has also written novelizations of movies. When she does this, she takes a screenplay and adds in new scenes to bridge gaps that are left by the film. She knows when tension needs to be added to a chapter. She knows when comedic relief will release the reader from the tension. She can also take a script or novel that needs clarifying and rework it to tell a beautiful story. She is brilliant at coming up with new plot twists to keep the reader guessing. Clearly, she is magic.

God is even more magical—or, I should say, miraculous. He is the ultimate Story Writer when we allow Him carte blanche with our stories. When we let Him do as many rewrites as possible, He will get our story exactly where He wants it. Just like Rene has the vision to reshape stories, God is reshaping ours. In my Albania story, He wanted to see if I was ready to trust Him. Would I still listen to Him when life was difficult? When I was struggling? When I faced my brokenness and had to relinquish my destructive coping mechanisms? Would I let Him lead me, in spite of my control issues? Could I do what He wanted me to do when I felt like my life was out of control, when I was scared and angry with extremely tight pants? Would I let Him finish the scene? Sometimes it is easier to read other people's stories than to actually *be* the story.

Bible Stories

My kids like to point out that some Bible stories are wildly inappropriate, which is true. Some of them are over-the-top gory. Some of them are just plain heartbreaking because these were real people. People who longed for a good life, who had different strengths and weaknesses. People who had made good, bad, and outright horrendous choices. And all of them were trying to figure it out. Life. Family. Love. Sorrow. Faith. They were no different than we are. They had the same struggles that we do. And they were hoping that God was going to write a good story on their behalf.

We can look at their stories and think, "Man, what a great decision!" or "Well, that was dumb. Why did he do that?" or "They really should do what God is asking them to do. It always works out better." And it is easy for us to think this because we know the whole story. But it is not so easy when we are living out our own stories. We long for control. We are hoping that God will give us the life we want. But if we think He might go off script (our script), we pull back from Him. We doubt Him. We think that maybe we should be the ones writing our story.

Life can only be understood backwards; but it must be lived forwards.

Søren Kierkegaard

Joseph's Story

Joseph sat alone, his back pressed against the hard wall of the prison. It was midnight. The air in the jail was stale and hot. Sweat trickled down his forehead. He never thought he would end up here. He was his dad's favorite. His mom's delight. He could see now that bragging about this to his older brothers wasn't his best move. Tears gathered in the corners of his eyes. Egypt was a long way from home. He thought he had hit rock bottom when his brothers sold him into slavery. But an Egyptian jail? He couldn't have seen it coming. Especially after he had worked so hard for Potiphar, trying to earn his favor. When Joseph was sold to him, he had swallowed his fear. He had gotten on with his life of service after being the one who was served for so many years. And now this. He couldn't even think about Potiphar's wife. She was such a liar. He kept replaying the look on Potiphar's face as he sent him away, full of anger and disappointment. Joseph was ruined.

God, where are you? Why am I here? What about those dreams you gave me? What do they even mean? Why is this happening to me? Joseph had tried so hard to be the man that God was calling him to be. He wanted to believe the dreams God had sent him about being a leader were real. But they seemed impossible now. Unthinkable. With the stench of prison surrounding him, they seemed like a cruel joke. All he wanted to do was go home to be with his mom and dad. With Benjamin. Putting his face in his hands, Joseph let the tears come.

This was the plot twist in Joseph's story. God had strategically placed him in that prison. He was learning how to be a servant leader. He was learning how to manage people. He was learning to listen for God's voice. He was learning to be attentive to those around him. All of these skills that he would need when he worked under Pharaoh, he learned in jail. Joseph was exactly where he was supposed to be, when he was supposed to be there, so that he could interpret the dreams of the baker and the wine taster. So that he could, in turn, interpret Pharaoh's dreams. So that he could be second in command in all of Egypt. So that he could provide food for Egypt and all the surrounding nations during a crucial time of famine. So that he could meet up with his brothers. And see Benjamin. And be with his family once again. His dream came true. His story just kept building and getting better. All of Joseph's hopes that were realized in that reunion moment began in prison. Best story ever.

The very least you can do in your life is figure out what you hope for. And the most you can do is live inside that hope. Not admire it from a distance but live right in it, under its roof.

Barbara Kingsolver

The Story of Hope

The story of Joseph is an amazing story. He lived an amazing life. It was a life written by the pen of the Master Storyteller. The same Master

Storyteller is singing a song of adventure over you. He can tell your story better than anyone. He gives dreams and restores relationships. He rewrites mistakes and rights wrongs. He is the script doctor who can take a tragedy and make it a triumph. He saves the best for last. All of His stories are love stories.

God's love for you is played out in the arc of your life, in the moments when you think your story is finished but He writes in a comeback. He pencils in light during your dark days. He works in miracle moments. He adds comfort and peace in scenes of deep grief. He edits out the permanence of death and foreshadows the great joy that lies ahead when you will see Him face-to-face. He wants to etch your story in grace and set it in hope. Most of all, He wants to give your story His ending, that is, eternity with Him. And there is no better ending than that.

I am writing your story.

CHAPTER 13

The Good Shepherd

When trouble comes, focus on God's ability to care for you.

Charles Stanley

Heartache and Pain

There are times in life that are so painful you think to yourself, *I am going to imagine myself in Hawaii, basking in the sun, and just pretend this isn't happening.* Sometimes it can actually work. But then there are the times when we are caught up in grief, and it so real and so present that we can hardly breathe. No imagining can change it. My friend Shelly was diagnosed with ovarian cancer four years ago. She fought so hard for a whole year. She fought for herself. She fought for her husband, Ben. She fought for her three kids, whom she loved more than life. And then her body decided that it was time to go home. The healing that needed to take place in her had to happen in heaven. Shelly was ready for that. But we weren't. We never really are when death comes to visit.

I had met Ben and Shelly when I started dating Scott during his youth-pastor years. Ben and Scott were best friends and were co-youth pastors together for eight years. We lived similar stories. Our lives were enmeshed with each other. Shelly was my good friend. My friend who understood everything about being married and in the ministry and about having three kids and working extra jobs to bring in income. We both planted churches around the same time. When they moved three hours north of us, we stayed close. We went to retreats together and found time to talk on the phone. She was the friend to whom I could tell anything, and we would laugh about it. When Shelly got sick, I went to work. I prayed. I fasted. I believed in my heart that God would heal her. He just had to. So when Ben called us a year into her illness and told us we needed to come say good-bye to Shelly, my world started breaking up, one little piece at a time. We packed our bags and put the kids in the car. I felt sick. Hope wasn't even an option. It seemed like all the goodness was being sucked out of life as we drove to the hospital.

When Scott and I walked into Shelly's hospital room, I started to cry. She was lying in bed not looking at all like herself. She was so sick. Then she said, "I love your purse. It's so cute." And there she was. The same Shelly as always. She looked at me and said, "Stop crying. I need you to make me laugh." So I wiped away my tears, put my cute purse down, and said, "Scott, say something funny." He is still upset with me that I put him on the spot. We stayed for five days. We laughed. We cried. We hugged. Shelly and I sang all the songs from all the musicals that we had been in together at church. She sang soprano. I sang alto. We reminisced about all the youth kids. Then we talked about Ben and how beautiful her kids were. But we didn't cry.

The morning before we had to leave, I stopped by the hospital to take Ben a cup of good coffee. Hospital coffee does not cut it in a crisis. He hugged me and said, "Go on in and say good-bye." I said, "I saw her last night. I don't want to interrupt her time with her dad." Her dad had driven in that morning to be with her. He raised his eyebrows and said, "Are you sure? I think you are going to want to see her one more time." I nodded and started crying. There was no more funny left in me. I peeked in the door of her room and told her dad, "I just want to say good-bye." Shelly saw my tears. She didn't ask me to make her laugh. I leaned down and cried into her neck and she said, "I'm going to see you in heaven." In the middle of her pain, she was comforting me. I said, "I know. I am just going to miss you so much. Just save me a place in the choir. I love you." "I love you, too." I kissed her on each cheek and practically sprinted out of the room. I couldn't stand it.

There was an ocean of wailing building up inside me. Out of the corner of my eye, I saw Ben crying, too, as I shot past him into an open elevator. I did a quick wave, but I avoided eye contact. There were two men inside the elevator. With tears pouring down my face, I looked at the two men and cried, pretty loudly, "I'm sooooo saaaaaaad." I was doing the ugly cry.

There was no holding back. At this point, the elevator door shut, and they were trapped with me. Now they looked sad. One of the men, who was sweating a little, nodded and said, "Yep. There are a lot of sad people here." The other one looked like he wished he had laser-beam eyes so he could cut a hole in the steel elevator door and escape. When the door did open, the men were gone in a flash. I have never seen two men move faster. I was undone. I knew that was the last time I would see my good friend, Shelly, here on earth. And I wasn't quite sure what to do with all feelings that I had.

I told Ben later, "I scared the guys in the elevator when I started crying." He laughed and said, "I know." I said, "You know?" He said, "The whole hospital floor heard you tell them how sad you were before the doors closed. It actually made me laugh." I was glad it made Ben laugh. Thank God we can cry and laugh at the same time in the darkness of despair. My awkward moment had given Ben some much-needed comic relief. We need all the light moments we can get when we are in pain. There is nothing that can prepare us for loss. There is nothing to quell the deep ache that throbs inside of us when we lose someone we love. Nothing. It is hard to find comfort in that place of pain.

There is a sacredness in tears. They are not the mark of weakness, but of power. They speak more eloquently than ten thousand tongues. They are the messengers of overwhelming grief, of deep contrition, and of unspeakable love.

Washington Irving

We all know that loss is a part of life. We know it. But knowing it is different than living it. Loss comes in all different shapes and sizes. Some of us have experienced tragedy in our own lives. We have watched our dreams die. We have lost family and friends. We have been shattered into a million pieces by the choices that others have made. We grieve the consequences of our own poor decisions, trapped in a place of pain. There are days when we feel like an open wound. We don't see how we will ever heal. Hope feels very, very far away. We are in the valley of the shadow of death. It is easy to lose heart there.

The darkest part of the valley for me was the hard pebble of doubt that buried itself in my soul. Maybe God wasn't good. Maybe He didn't care. I didn't voice my doubts. I just pondered them in my heart, like sharp little rocks that cut me every time I turned them over. I made an appointment with my counselor. I told her, "I am going back into depression. I can feel it." She told me gently, "No, Susanna, you are just grieving." I argued, "I really think I am depressed." She put her hand on my arm. "You are going to be OK, but this is a process. I have a grief group that I think would be good for you to attend." I didn't want to go to grief group. I wanted to Shelly to be alive. I sat on the couch in her office and cried, a ball of tissues in my lap. "Well, this is horrible." And it was. Grief is, in general.

Knowing that I was feeling a tiny portion of what Ben and the kids were feeling made me feel even crazier. There was nothing I could do to help them feel better. I couldn't even make myself feel better. I tried to remind myself that compared to some, my grief was minimal, wasn't it? All over the world were millions who had experienced heartrending tragedy. Scores of people are caught up in loss and grief on a daily basis. People are hurting and alone. But somehow that just made it worse. If this was what life was going to be like from here on out, I wondered, where was God? Where did He go? Were we abandoned in our suffering? Did He see all of us? Did He hear us? What was He going do about all this sadness? All this loss? All this pain?

The LORD is my shepherd, I lack nothing.

He makes me lie down in green pastures,
he leads me beside quiet waters,
he refreshes my soul.
He guides me along the right paths
for his name's sake.
Even though I walk
through the darkest valley,
I will fear no evil,
for you are with me;
your rod and your staff,
they comfort me.

Psalm 23:1-4 NIV

David's Grief

King David wasn't a stranger to suffering or despair. He understood grief. He had experienced loss. In fact, David had experienced every loss imaginable. He had felt the loss of his best friend, Jonathan. The loss of favor of Jonathan's dad, Saul. The death of his marriage to Michal, Saul's daughter. The self-inflicted grief of living with the consequences of his own sins of murder and adultery. The loss of his and Bathsheba's first child. The rape of his daughter at the hands of his own son. The revenge murder of that son by his younger son, Absalom. The death of Absalom when he tried to overthrow David and become king. What kind of grief did David not endure? Grief upon grief. Loss upon horrendous loss. How was he not a complete and total wreck?

Here is a man who should have been broken in half by the weight of his grief. He should have been shattered in a thousand pieces by his experiences. But instead, his songs of lament were punctuated with praise. He sang of God's majesty and justness and rightness. David praised God for all that He had done for him. Along with his tearful cries for help, he spoke out about his belief in God's goodness and about the God who rescued him. David knew the heart of God. He knew that it was turned toward those who were suffering. When he was in pain, David went looking for the One who could comfort him. He went looking for the Good Shepherd.

But now, Lord, what do I look for?
My hope is in you.

Psalm 39:7 NIV

What Is a Shepherd?

God was and is the Good Shepherd. Drawing David near. Healing his wounds. Guarding his heart. Directing his path. Giving him good footing. Providing him with rest. Quieting his hurting heart. Bringing moments of grace and refreshment in the midst of David's pain. When David referred to God as his shepherd, he knew what being a shepherd meant. David had been a shepherd for years.

He knew what it was to part the sheep's rough wool with his staff to seek out the hurts and cuts of his flock. He understood how to protect them from roaming predators with the stout rod in his hand. He knew how to pick a safe path down a rocky ledge, making sure every sheep was safe. When they ran from him in fear, he knew how to use the crook of his staff to pull the sheep to safety.[1]

David had gathered his flock close daily. He had soothed their bleats with the steadiness of his voice a thousand times. David knew a good shepherd when he saw one. And he recognized the touch of the Good Shepherd in his own life. He felt himself being drawn close in moments of pain and fear. He saw God providing his every need. He sensed God protecting him from harm. He knew that God was hearing his every cry of pain and sorrow and that He was responding to it each and every time.

The LORD is close to the brokenhearted
and saves those who are crushed in spirit.

Psalm 34:18 NIV

Hope Brings Comfort

God is not immune to our suffering here on earth. He sees the pain that we endure. He hears our cries. He meets us in the midst of our suffering and pulls us out of our pain, bringing comfort and healing. There is hope to be found in His arms. There is solace in His words of affirmation and understanding. *I love you. I know how you feel. I've got you. I am never letting you go. This will get better.* God is singing a song of comfort over us. A shepherd's song. The one about His loving-kindness and how there is healing in His hands. It is time to lean in.

The Shepherd loves you in your brokenness. He will love you through your tears. He will love you through your loss. And you can know beyond the shadow of a doubt that He is good.

I am your comforter.

CHAPTER 14
The Warrior King

We are armed twice if we fight with faith.

Plato

Love Karate and Flashbangs

My husband, Scott, is a black belt. It was one of the many interesting attributes that attracted me to him in college. Before we began dating, I would ask him to show me different blocks. My friend, Leslie, called this "love karate." She said I was just asking him to show me moves so that I could be close to him. I will neither confirm nor deny this accusation. But I was an attentive student. You might want to fear me a little. Just know that if you sneak up and grab me from behind, I will either crush your instep with my heel or donkey kick you in your nether regions. So tread lightly, my friend. Love karate is powerful stuff.

Scott took Shorinji Tae Gar, a hybrid of eight different styles of martial arts, for six years. He went to class every day. He graduated to teaching the younger classes. He excelled at katas, the choreographed motions used to practice different martial arts movements. The motions became so familiar that they were like breathing to him. He is trained so that if he is ever in the position where he needs to fight, he doesn't think. He just responds. I am trained so that if I ever need to fight, I freak out, scream, and try to run. Not a horrible response, but not the best way to fight.

When our son, Will, found his dad's martial arts weaponry hidden in a closet a few years ago, he looked at Scott in awe, like he had just realized he had been living with a ninja all along. Scott went up a few notches in Will's estimation. All of Scott's ninja training came into play last December. You may be thinking, isn't your husband a pastor? Yes. He is. A black-belt pastor. We were sitting in our living room, and I had just asked our boys to go outside and take the trash cans to the curb. Scott heard some commotion and said, "Boys, wait a second; I want to check something out." He went outside for a few minutes and came back in. What he heard were police helicopters circling overhead. There was a search going on.

Scott had checked in with our neighbor only to find out that we had missed the phone tree message from the police station since we no longer have a landline. There was a murder suspect on the loose. He was considered armed and dangerous. The elementary school down the street had been set up as a base for the police's tactical team to work from. We had been advised to barricade ourselves into our homes. With the looming sound of choppers overhead and search lights flickering past our windows, we tried to stay calm. We began to pray. And Scott went into warrior mode.

Out came the hidden sais from the closet. These are martial arts weapons used in blocking and deflecting swords. Kitchen knives also were pulled out, along with an incredibly sharp blender blade that makes me nervous every time I make a smoothie. Chairs were placed around the house in strategic positions. I was in charge of keeping the children calm, which is interesting since my heart was thundering in my chest like a bass drum. Scott secured the house, putting wedges in the doors and pieces of wood up to brace the windows. He said, "Sue, if he gets inside, you take the boys and run. Call 911." He could not have been more serious. As we peeked through the shades in Scott's office, we could see the police searching the bushes. One stood in our front yard. This was no joke. And I can assure you that no one was laughing.

About an hour and a half into the lockdown, two explosions rattled our windows. We found out later that these were "flashbangs," or non-exploding grenades used to stun and frighten but not harm. They worked. We were stunned and frightened. We moved the boys into Jack's bedroom, which had the least number of windows, and kept them distracted with screens. I was texting my family and friends to pray. Scott was following the police updates on his phone to keep apprised of the situation. The suspect was apprehended four hours after the ordeal began. He was holed up in a home four houses down and across the street from ours.

We have never in our life been more thankful for our local police and their collective experience. I was thankful for Scott. The preacher man with the sais who has a cool head in a crisis, who was ready to defend our family if it came to that. Love karate in action. And I was thankful for the One who battles for my family every day. The One who has angel armies at the ready. The One who hears every single prayer that we pray and wages war in heaven on our behalf. The struggle is real, and God is on our side.

Fight:
Battle. Warfare. Skirmish. Combat. Engage.

Spiritual Warfare

There is a very real battle going on around us every day. We may or may not be aware of it, but it requires our attention. God wants us in on the fight. He has called us to a daily spiritual battle. I don't think that demons lurk around every corner and that every bad thing that happens in life is because of the devil. But I do know that the enemy is real. To deny it is foolishness. And in the Bible, it says that the enemy's main mission is to steal, kill, and destroy. He is not fond of those whom God has created. If he can, he will take us all out at the knees. He will work against whatever good thing God is doing in our lives. He leaves chaos and pain in his wake. He is the enemy of our souls.

The first step on the way to victory is recognize the enemy.

Corrie ten Boom

God is calling us to be aware. To guard our hearts and our minds against the enemy's attacks. And to lift up our brothers and sisters in Jesus to Him. He doesn't want us to be caught up in the enemy's schemes. We get to have an active role in this battle. Not with sais and blender blades, but with arrows of prayers, petitions, and praise. These are the weapons that cripple the work of the enemy. Prayer and worship give us our chance to take him out at the knees.

Finally, be strong in the Lord and in his mighty power. Put on the full armor of God, so that you can take your stand against the devil's schemes. For our struggle is not against flesh and blood, but against the rulers, against the authorities, against the powers of this dark world and against the spiritual forces of evil in the heavenly realms.

Ephesians 6:10-12 NIV

The good news is that God is leading us into this spiritual battle. And He is way more powerful than the enemy of our souls. There is no comparison between the two. God can out-scheme, out-maneuver, and out-flank the enemy on all sides. When Elisha, the prophet, was advising the king of Israel in the battle against the king of Aram, he knew the truth. He could see what was going on in the spiritual realm. He knew God was on their side. Elisha's servant, however, could only see that they were surrounded on every side by the enemy. The servant thought the King of Aram was winning the battle. Second Kings 6:15-17 (NIV) tells the story:

> When the servant of the man of God got up and went out early the next morning, an army with horses and chariots had surrounded the city. "Oh no, my lord! What shall we do?" the servant asked. "Don't be afraid," the prophet answered. "Those who are with us are more than those who are

> with them." And Elisha prayed, "Open his eyes, LORD, so that he may see." Then the LORD opened the servant's eyes, and he looked and saw the hills full of horses and chariots of fire all around Elisha.

Elisha knew that God was inviting them to a battle He had already won. God's creativity and resources are beyond anything that we can imagine. His power is unmatched. His army will always win. There is no contest. We need to fight knowing God is on our side. And He is the one who brings the victory.

Do not be afraid of them; the LORD your God himself will fight for you.

Deuteronomy 3:22 NIV

Gwen's Story

Gwen held the cablegram in her shaky hand. How could this be happening? She felt helpless. Her husband, Oliver, was overseas at the Bible school that they had started in the south of India. Even though their missionary term wasn't complete, she and their two children, Louanne and Dick, had returned home to the States, due to sickness. The cablegram was asking for prayer. The principal of the school was on his deathbed. He was a good man, and they needed him to continue the work in India after Oliver left. How could the school survive without his leadership? This news was almost more than Gwen could bear.

Nothing about missionary life in India had been easy for Gwen. She had faced depression, illness, and the near death of their four-year-old son to malaria. At every turn, there had been opposition and difficulty, from the unbearable poverty that surrounded them to the separation from family and friends. This was compounded by the culture shock of living abroad. But one thing she had learned in her time overseas was to pray. Prayer was something she had leaned into. It was her lifeline in every difficulty that she faced. As she prayed, she knew God had fought alongside her every step of the way.

Gwen picked up the phone. She called several churches and asked them to pray. She called the women at her church and asked for their prayers. Then she hit her knees. She prayed for hours. Even though she was tired. She prayed until she felt a lifting in her spirit and the reassurance that God was on the move. Halfway around the world, the principal of the school was in dire straits. His family had been with him all day. He was dying. Two students from the school offered to let the family rest and stayed in the room keeping vigil throughout the night. They prayed for healing. For God's mighty hand to work a miracle. They were desperate. They were doing what they could to join the fight and pray for the healing of this good man. While they were praying, they both had a vision of men dressed in white surrounding the principal, with swords raised to the sky, forming a canopy over the bed. Above the pointed tips of the swords, they saw dark forms swirling. The forms were held back by the swords. They were held back by the mighty hand of God and the prayers that were going up around the world. The principal was miraculously healed.

A week later when Gwen read this miracle story in Oliver's letter, she was floored. God was not held back by time or space or distance. Prayer had unleashed God's power in a miraculous way in that room halfway around the world. She may have been far away from the crisis, but in that moment, God used her prayers to bring a spiritual victory. She had joined the fight, and the fight had been won. The power of prayer isn't the stuff of legends. It is the stuff of today. It is real. It works. My grandma, Gwen, was a strong woman who believed in a stronger God. Her prayers, along with those of her friends, changed the course of history.

Devote yourselves to prayer, being watchful and thankful.

Colossians 4:2 NIV

A King Who Fights

God is inviting us to a spiritual battle. And He has stacked the odds in our favor with His power. His wisdom. His strength. His healing. His input. But we have to engage. We have to ask for His help and intervention. We have to pray. His plans for this earth and for humanity always include us. He is all-powerful, but He uses us to show His power. He uses our weakness to reveal His strength. He is all-knowing, but He uses us to speak His truth. His loving-kindness is unstoppable, but He uses us to touch those around us with His love, His grace, and His peace. We are the prayer warriors, and He is the Warrior King. Leading us. Guiding us. Directing us. Bringing the shock and awe, as it were.

The One who knows the enemy inside and out intervenes in supernatural ways every day. We don't always see it happening. We are like Elisha's servant. We think the other side is winning. With our limited vision, it is easy to grow discouraged and feel like prayer is a small thing. Like our words don't make a difference. But the Warrior King loves words. He spoke the universe into existence using words. He calmed the seas with words. He breathed life back into the dead with words. He can do anything He wants to with words.

Our words and our prayers matter to Him. They always have. Our hope rests in the fact that He doesn't expect us to battle on our own. Our hope grows when we pray and recognize that He is fighting alongside us. Our hopes are realized when we hear that He is singing a song of protection over us. It is His battle cry. He sings out against evil and despair and hatred. Against sickness and persecution and poverty. His heart is for the poor and the downtrodden. His aim is for restoration, forgiveness, and healing. His ear is turned toward the words of the ones He loves. And He is fighting on our behalf.

I am fighting for you.

CHAPTER 15

The Faithful Friend

There is nothing on this earth more to be prized than true friendship.

Thomas Aquinas

A True Friend

My dad always says, "We are designed for relationship." We are created with a deep need for intimacy. We need friendship with our Creator. And we need friendship with one another. Having a true friend is something that doesn't just happen. It requires a commitment by both parties, saying, "I am going to stick with you. No matter what." And it is the "no matter what" part that truly puts a friendship to the test.

During my downward spiral during my junior year in college, when I walked away from God, I also walked away from my friends. I had a close group of girlfriends that I had started college with. We were inseparable. But then they wouldn't support me in my poor decision making. They kept calling me on my choices, asking me things like, "What are you doing?" and saying things like, "We think you are better than this." So I decided I was better off without them. I would much rather struggle with an eating disorder, maintain questionable relationships, and fail my classes than admit that they were right. Clearly, I had issues. But I thought I knew what I was doing. What I didn't know was what they were doing.

My girlfriends were meeting behind my back. Talking about me. To Jesus. They held secret prayer meetings for me. I was ignoring them. And they were bringing my name before the God of the Universe. I was telling them that they didn't know what was best for me. And they were asking God to show me His best for me. Asking Him to bring me close. To show me His goodness and mercy. To open my eyes to the path I was walking down without Him. They were tethering me to the truth with their prayers. I gave up on them. But they never gave up on me.

The morning that I woke up and realized that I had become a person who had to make herself sick to feel good, I realized three things: (1) I didn't know who I was anymore, (2) I needed Jesus, and (3) I missed my friends. When I told my parents what was going on, I knew, on some level, that they would always love me, no matter what. We had that family bond. But the bonds of friendship can be more tenuous. Friends aren't family. Friends choose one another. I had unchosen my dearest friends. What would they do?

It was the end of the school year. I called each one of them and let them know what was going on. That I was moving in with my aunt and uncle. That I was battling an eating disorder. That I wouldn't be coming back to school in the fall. That I would be going to a counselor. That I was broken. And that I was sorry. Sorry for how I had shut them out. For how I hadn't listened to their words of love and advice. For all my dumbness. So, so, very sorry. And each friend listened and then said, "Sue, I forgive you." I broke down weeping each time those words were said to me.

I forgive you. Those are words of hope and light in a dark place. They are the words of a faithful friend. One who sees who you are now but knows that is not who you will always be. These girls were showing me the breadth and width and depth of what it meant to be a friend. I had failed them. But they were choosing me anyway. Choosing to love me. To engage with me. To hope with me. To pray with me. It changed my life. It changed me. I was never the same after that.

A real friend is one who walks in when the rest
of the world walks out.

Walter Winchell

Peter's Story

The waves sloshed up against the side of the boat. The scent of fish guts and wet rope surrounded Peter. He sat slumped against the hull, head in his hands. He didn't have any tears left. It had been a hard night fishing. It had been an even harder month. Mind-boggling and confusing. Losing Jesus had ripped him apart. His dearest friend. His leader. His hope. It had shattered all the disciples in different ways. Some of them had gone back to fishing to clear their heads. John tugged at the nets, checking to see if any fish had found their way in. None. None all night.

Peter replayed the scenes of the last few weeks over and over again in his mind. Passover. The crowds cheering for Jesus. The dark night of prayer in the garden when he couldn't keep his eyes open. Judas's kiss of betrayal. His fear and anger boiling over as he sliced off the guard's ear with his sword. The jaw-dropping moment when Jesus calmly put the ear back on the guard, completely healing it. Then came the worst part. Denying Jesus in the courtyard. And the look on Jesus' face when the cock crowed three times. The crowds calling for his blood. The Crucifixion. The earthquakes. It felt like the end of the world.

The Resurrection. That had been something altogether different. Peter had seen the empty tomb himself. Jesus was gone. Or was He? Had He actually risen from the dead? Each time He appeared to them seemed unreal. In the middle of a locked room, how was that possible? Was He real? Was He a ghost? What did He think of them and how they had acted during His darkest hours? Did He still love them? Had He forgiven them?

Peter was having a hard time forgiving himself. That was for sure. There was the gut-wrenching guilt that was eating him alive. Knowing that he had done exactly what Jesus said he would do. Denying him outright. He had been swallowed by fear when that girl asked him if he knew Jesus. He blurted out "no" before he could think twice. How could he have denied Jesus? After all they had been through together? Peter rubbed a coarse sleeve across his forehead. If only he could do those last days over again. He would have owned up to knowing Jesus. He would have taken whatever punishment they gave him. He would have tried to speak up on his behalf. At least, he would have been brave enough to stay at the cross like John had. Instead, he ran. He felt like he was still running.

The sun was creeping into the early morning sky, throwing out rays of pink and yellow. A call came from the shore. "Friends, haven't you any fish?" There was something familiar about that voice. Peter stood up and looked out across the water at the beach. Shading his eyes against the rising sun, he tried to make out who it was. The man called out again, "Throw your net on the right side of the boat, and you will find some." At his direction, they hauled up the nets and threw them over the other side of the boat.

Immediately, the weight of the fish yanked on the nets, pulling them down. Leaning near the water, they grabbed onto the nets with both hands. Silvery fish flipped water into their faces. Laugher broke out. John lit up. He grinned at Peter and said, "It is the Lord!" Peter didn't think twice. He dropped the net, grabbed his coat, and hit the water with a splash. Jesus was back, and He had called him friend.

Then the disciple whom Jesus loved said to Peter, "It is the Lord!" As soon as Simon Peter heard him say, "It is the Lord," he wrapped his outer garment around him (for he had taken it off) and jumped into the water. The other disciples followed in the boat, towing the net full of fish, for they were not far from shore, about a hundred yards. When they landed, they saw a fire of burning coals there with fish on it, and some bread. Jesus said to them, "Bring some of the fish you have just caught." So Simon Peter climbed back into the boat and dragged the net ashore. It was full of large fish, 153, but even with so many the net was not torn. Jesus said to them, "Come and have breakfast." None of the disciples dared ask him, "Who are you?"

They knew it was the Lord. Jesus came, took the bread and gave it to them, and did the same with the fish. This was now the third time Jesus appeared to his disciples after he was raised from the dead.

John 21:7-14 NIV

What a True Friend Looks Like

A true friend looks and sounds and acts a whole lot like Jesus. Jesus could have showed up at the beach and said, "Man, you guys are a huge disappointment. I thought you were my friends. You really messed up in the garden. You deserted me at the cross. You denied me. After all I have done for you? Unbelievable." All of these things would have been true. The last time they had broken bread together was at the Passover. Jesus had talked about heaven. He had talked about His Father. And He had talked about friendship. Jesus had told them, "Greater love has no one than this: to lay down one's life for one's friends. You are my friends if you do what I command. I no longer call you servants, because a servant does not know his master's business. Instead, I have called you friends, for everything that I learned from my Father I have made known to you" (John 15:13-15 NIV).

He then proceeded to do just what He said. He laid down His life for His friends. Literally. And they had scattered. Scared. Anxious. Uncertain of what the future held for them.

Friend:
Ally. Companion. Confidante. Intimate. Soul mate.

When Jesus showed up on the beach that morning, He wasn't just offering broiled fish and toasty bread. He was offering do-overs and second chances. He was affirming them and showing them their future as Christ-followers. As he prepared a meal of miracle fish, He was saying, in essence, "Let's give this one more shot. The last time we ate dinner together it didn't go down so well. I want to show you how friendship is supposed to work." Friendship is steeped in love. Loaded with forgiveness. And chock full of grace. Jesus wasn't saying, "What you did didn't matter." He was saying, "What you did mattered, but I know that is not who you are. Let's have breakfast and work this out."

Jesus was showing them what it looks like to be a faithful friend. The friend who never gives up on you. The friend who shows up in the darkest moments of life and brings hope and more hope. He knew his disciples inside and out. He could see the shame written on Peter's face. But He knew who Peter was going to be. Who He had created him to be. He knew that Peter was a man whose faith was going to change the destiny of the world. He wanted Peter to know that, too. He saw the disciples in their suffering and in their loss that morning and shouted across the water, "Friends!" That miracle breakfast of fish on the beach wasn't just about feeding empty bellies. It was about Jesus choosing His disciples one more time. He was choosing to love them. To engage with them. To pray for them. To change them. And He was inviting them to do the same for everyone they came in contact with.

When they had finished eating, Jesus said to Simon Peter, "Simon son of John, do you love me more than these?"

"Yes, Lord," he said, "you know that I love you."

Jesus said, "Feed my lambs."

Again Jesus said, "Simon son of John, do you love me?"

He answered, "Yes, Lord, you know that I love you."

Jesus said, "Take care of my sheep."
The third time he said to him, "Simon son of John, do you love me?"
Peter was hurt because Jesus asked him the third time, "Do you love me?" He said, "Lord, you know all things; you know that I love you."
Jesus said, "Feed my sheep."

John 21:15-17 NIV

Jesus is inviting us into His inner circle. We get a giant taste of hope when we realize that He is singing a song of friendship over us. It is a meet-Me-on-the-beach-for-breakfast kind of song. He is choosing us again. He knows we have not always been faithful to Him. We may have disappointed Him. But He also knows who He created us to be: His friend. His comrade in arms. His hands of love and grace extended. He is choosing to love us. To engage us. To challenge us. In turn, He wants us to do the same to those around us. He wants us to care for His kids, His sheep. When we choose friendship with Jesus and His kids, everyone wins. Forgiveness abounds. Encouragement is on the rise. And love—the real kind—shows up. There He is. Love incarnate. Jesus is showing up today and calling out to us by name, "Friends!" And it doesn't get any better than that.

I am your faithful friend.

CHAPTER 16

The Hope of Heaven

Do not abandon yourselves to despair.
We are the Easter people and hallelujah is our song.

Pope John Paul II

Easter Joy

Easter Sunday is my favorite Sunday of the year. As a child, I could barely sleep the night before. Easter always involved a new dress, candy, and cousins. It was a huge mash up of joy. Most of my Easter Sundays were spent in Modesto at my Grandpa Blakeley's church. A bunch of us cousins would cram into a pew, passing notes, coming down off of the peanut-butter-cup sugar rush from our candy-filled baskets. We stood shoulder-to-shoulder sharing the hymnals, trying to out sing each other, the louder the better. Aunt Neva would be making the organ swell, and we matched her volume.

The choir always sang on Easter. If we were lucky, Uncle Carl and Aunt Lana would be singing solos. It was easy to sing Easter hymns loudly. They call for it! The louder the song, the more majestic we felt. You could feel the excitement in the air. And it wasn't just all the extra sugar we had eaten. I may not have understood the Resurrection theology on those Sundays, but the hymn lyrics that trumpeted His rising from the dead moved my child's heart.

"Up from the Grave He Arose." "Christ the Lord Has Risen Today." "He Lives! He Lives!" "Alive! Alive! Alive! Forevermore!" "Death Had Lost Its Sting." "Nothing Could Keep Jesus Down." "Victory in Jesus!" I knew something magnificent had gone down on Easter. It had shifted the lives of those around me. It changed them. It changed the looks on their faces. And I wanted in on that excitement. I still feel that excitement on Easter morning, even though there is no sugar to pump me up. Now I go in for coffee. And these days I am not caught up in the swell of the organ; I am surrounded by the joy of children in our kids' class at church.

We share the Easter Story. We sing songs, and we like the loud ones. We do our best to shout praise to Jesus. We make crafts and talk about what Easter is all about. The amazingness of it. The great surprise of death being overcome. The empty tomb. The glorious angels. The hugeness of what Jesus did for us in that moment. I don't know if they understand the theology of Easter, but they have the same looks on their faces that I did as a child. Joy. Wonder. Excitement. The good stuff.

This year I asked my nephew, Drew, who is six, if he would share the Easter story using his Resurrection eggs that he had gotten at school. Each plastic egg held a different piece of the Easter story. Drew said, "Yep." He was the envy of all the kids in the class. Who wouldn't want twelve plastic Easter eggs filled with tiny reminders of the Easter story? The tiny piece of cord for the whip that Jesus was wounded with and the thorn for the crown of thorns brought a lot of interest. It was Easter told in miniature, but it had a big effect.

Drew did an amazing job sharing the story, despite several interruptions from a zealous three-year-old who kept opening the eggs before their time. He gently instructed his small friend, "That is number five. We are on number two." And when the tiny stone that represented the stone that sealed the tomb was released with great joy, Drew said, "Please put back number 11. I'm not ready for it." The excitement was ramping up. The kids were all leaning forward to see what the last egg was. They knew that Jesus had suffered and died on the cross. They knew that the stone had been rolled away. What would be next? With great anticipation, Drew cracked open the last egg. It was empty. The kids crowded forward, mesmerized, waiting to hear the explanation of the empty egg. I asked, "What happened? Why is the egg empty?" One of the kindergarteners answered in a loud whisper, "He escaped!"

And there it was. He escaped. The great theme of every Easter anthem that has ever been written. Jesus wasn't dead! He was alive! They went looking for Him, and He was gone. He pulled a fast one on the devil. That dark ending to all of humanity's story wasn't the ending to Jesus' story. When death came for Him, He gave it the slip. He was and is unconquerable. Unmatched. Jesus is so powerful that He died and came back to life. He was the Death Defier. The Divine Healer. The Escape Artist. All rolled into one. He is unstoppable, unchangeable, and undefeatable. It is the best story of all time. And more than that? It isn't a story. It really happened. Jesus came back from the dead, and we will never be the same.

On the first day of the week, very early in the morning, the women took the spices they had prepared and went to the tomb. They found the stone rolled away from the tomb, but when they entered, they did not find the body of the Lord Jesus. While they were wondering about this, suddenly two men in clothes that gleamed like lightning stood beside them. In their fright the women bowed down with their faces to the ground, but the men said to them, "Why do you look for the living among the dead? He is not here; he has risen! Remember how he told you, while he was still with you in Galilee: 'The Son of Man must be delivered over to the hands of sinners, be crucified and on the third day be raised again.'"

Luke 24:1-7 NIV

Resurrection Ruth

I can't imagine what it must have been like for disciples to lose everything when Jesus was crucified. To have the hopes of their coming Messiah dashed and to lose their leader and friend must have crushed them. But my family has known a small taste of what the disciples felt that Resurrection morning so long ago. When hope beyond hope was restored. When their greatest dreams were realized. The amazement. The throwing off of grief. The joy of one more day in the presence of a loved one.

Three years ago my mom, Ruth, was on a retreat with my dad and a few close friends. While she was sitting on the couch, she took a deep breath, and then she was gone. She experienced sudden cardiac death. Within minutes, the police and paramedics were working on her heart, resuscitating her, cooling down her body with ice packs, and whisking her away to be airlifted to a cardiac center. A seemingly normal day turned into our worst nightmare. We kids flew in from California, Oregon, and Hawaii. She was in an induced coma, letting her body and mind recover from the ordeal. She was hooked up to monitors and machines and a ventilator. Her eyes were closed.

When we walked into her room, the full force of what had happened hit us. I began to cry. All of the things that made her my mom—her laughter, her smile, the way that she loved us and hugged us and said our names—were locked up somewhere else far away. We stood in the room, touching her hands, kissing her face, letting her know how much we wanted her to please come back. To be with us. The doctors had told my dad that either, "She could wake up with brain damage. She could wake up and be OK. Or she might not wake up at all." What he didn't tell us were the impossible odds that Mom was facing. About one in ten survive what she was going through.

We were all in shock. Dad wouldn't leave my mom's side. We crowded into the family waiting rooms. Waiting. Hoping. Praying. Praying for a miracle that only the One who had known resurrection himself could bring. And the world was stripped down to two emotions: love and fear. They filled us up. I realized in that crystallized moment of time how much I love the woman who birthed me and how scared I was that I would never hear her say my name again. As we crowded into that hospital room where she lay, we found that we couldn't stand the fear. It sucked the air from the room and left us weeping. But the love part, that is what gave us words.

Telling her who she was, what she meant to us, how we knew she needed to rest, but come Friday morning when they brought her out of sedation, she was going to need to wake up and come back to us.

My mom always lights a candle on the kitchen counter whenever someone needs prayer. The flickering light reminds her to pray for them throughout the day. All around the world friends and family lit candles and lifted up prayers for Mom. They posted pictures of the candles on social media. Those prayers and pictures bolstered us up and held us in that place of love. The waiting seemed unbearable. As I tried to wrap up in a hospital blanket on a hard couch to catch a few minutes of sleep, I couldn't find words to match the depth of what I was feeling. My prayers were distilled down to one word: *please*. To the God of heaven who holds life and breath in His hands. *Please. Please. Please.* In the hospital with my family, by her bed, kissing her hands, touching her face, praying for one more day to see her and know her here on earth. *Please.*

Around midnight on Thursday, the nurse convinced us kids that we needed to go home and sleep for a few hours. Since they were going to start weaning Mom off of the paralytic around 5:00 a.m. on Friday, we should come back then. Dad stayed with Mom, and a dear friend sat in the room with him. We piled our weary selves into cars and went to a friend's house to get a few hours of sleep. Then came the call at 2:00 a.m. that upended our world and lit us up. My sister, Erica, threw open the door to my room. After two hours of sleep I was hardly coherent. "Sue! Wake up! Mom is waking up!"

"What?"

"Mom is awake in the hospital!" To say there were screams of joy was an understatement. We threw open Jenny's door, the light from the hallway nearly blinding her. "Jenny, wake up! Mom is awake!"

"What?!"

"Yes! She's awake!" Mom came out of the coma on her own, and we pretty much lost our minds with joy. We were jumping up and down, hugging one another and weeping. I busted out a few sweet dance moves. This is what resurrection felt like. Death to life. Sorrow to joy. Despair to hope in a single moment.

Mom was coming back to us, her eyes open, breathing on her own, wiggling her toes. A bona fide miracle in the wee morning hours. And in that moment of unbelievable joy, my prayer of *please* shifted to *thank You. Thank You. Thank You. Thank You. Thank You.* The Scripture I read the morning my mom woke up was Psalm 50:14-15 (NLT):

> *What I want instead is your true thanks to God;*
> *I want you to fulfill your vows to the Most High.*
> *Trust me in your times of trouble*
> *and I will rescue you,*
> *and you will give me glory.*

Every nerve in my body was singing a song of thanksgiving. We knew what Mary and Martha felt like when Lazarus took his first step out of the grave. In the wee hours of the morning, when Dad, Erica, Jenny, Chris, and I gathered around Mom's bed, we were standing on holy ground. Mom was a miracle. She says that the people who began praying for her when she went down were the first responders on the scene. Thousands of people began lifting her up in prayer, asking for her life to be given back to her. To us. A thundering cry went up to heaven on her behalf. And in all of His power, Jesus shouted back across the universe, "Yes!" Yes to new life in my Mom's body. Yes to more days on earth. Yes to healing in her mind and body. Yes to waking her up at 2:00 in the morning and sending us into a frenzy of joy.

When Mom woke up, it was a fulfillment of hope. A taste of what heaven will be like here on earth. Buoyed by the love and prayers of thousands that went up on Mom's behalf, we saw the glory of the Lord in a real and palpable way. She is here with us because He made it so. That is the only reason.

Resurrection:
Rebirth. Resurgence. Restoration. Revival. Return to life.

Jesus is the Resurrection and the Life. When He shook off the grave clothes and stepped into the early morning light on that first Easter morning, it was more than just a miracle. It sent a ripple of hope through all of eternity. All that had been wrong since the first moment of sin had been forgiven. Jesus was not only alive but also bringing light and life to each of us. Through His death and resurrection, He was giving us a new chance at living. Our own rebirth story. Because He lives, He has given us a path for healing. He has paved the way to escape the darkness of death. Heaven is now in our sights. Life with Him for all of eternity is our new ending. He is singing a resurrection song over us. A song of life reborn.

Jesus' love is so strong and wide and deep, we can't fathom it. He is still in the resurrection business. It's Easter every day as far as He is concerned. He is breathing life back into dead dreams and dying relationships. He is stopping death in its tracks, bringing healing to broken bodies and broken minds. He is restoring marriages, reuniting mothers and fathers to their children, and then some. He is bringing new life and new hope to every person that He touches. He wants to restore us completely. God has death-defying plans for us. Plans for rebirth, second chances, new life, and ultimately a life in heaven with Him. The greatest escape of all.

It is time to throw off every fear and every doubt and realize that Jesus isn't just singing hope over us; He is our hope. He is looking for us to share the hope of who He is with everyone around us. It's not too late to start spreading that love around. It needs to be trumpeted from every mountaintop and sung into the valleys. It needs to shouted across the waters and carried to the every man, woman, and child. Are you ready to hope? Are you ready for the adventure of a lifetime? Are you ready to sing His song at the top of your lungs? Hope is our great calling. We have known the power of the Resurrection and freedom from the fear of death. We are the Easter people. And hallelujah is our song.

I am hope.

Hope Sings . . .

Don't be afraid.

Just believe.

I love you.

I am singing over you.

I am setting you free.

I am redeeming you.

I am calming your storm.

I am always on time.

I am writing your story.

I am your comforter.

I am fighting for you.

I am your faithful friend.

I am hope.

CHAPTER 17

Risk More. Dream Bigger. Fear Less.

Never be afraid to trust an unknown future to a known God.

Corrie ten Boom

Living Out Hope

Life has a way of changing things up on you. When I came back to Bible college after leaving my junior year, I had one semester left before graduation. I was ready for a new adventure. My plan was to follow up my graduation with an internship in New York City at Time Square Church. I wanted to experience life to the fullest. I wanted to do more for God after all He had done for me. It was a new season. Bright and shiny. All I had to do was graduate.

I was focused on good grades and having fun with my girlfriends when I got back to school. I had sworn off of boys. When I had been in Hawaii at the discipleship training school, the only boy I would hang out with was my cousin-to-be, Josh. Mostly because I didn't trust myself with making good relationship choices. When one of the guys in the school told my friend, "I asked Susanna if she wanted to hang out, and she said, 'No thanks. I'm not friends with boys.'" It was true. I had decided that I was done with liking guys. At least until I met the one God had for me. I had made a list of thirty-two different qualities that I wanted in the next boy that I liked. No one I met in the year following my discipleship training school came close.

Enter Scott. A youth pastor who led a rap ministry. He had started school the year after I left. He wasn't my type at all, and I wasn't his. We were about the same height. He had blonde hair and blue eyes. My list stated that the next boy I liked would be 6'2" and have brown hair and green eyes. Scott usually liked petite girls with lots of personality. But he was funny. And I was funny. And we made each other laugh. So we started hanging out. We would eat lunch together. And check our mail together. I found myself looking for him on campus. And thinking about him in class. It was craziness. This was not the plan.

During homecoming week, all the classes met at the park for an all-class relay race. Scott and I were standing next to each other, waiting for our turn to run, and our friend, Brett, said, "Hey, dude! She's taller than you." Scott said, "No, she's not." And I said, "Am I?" And Scott said, "Let's go back-to-back." So we kicked off our shoes and stood back-to-back. Brett measured us with his hand. We were almost exactly the same height. And I turned and faced Scott and said, "How tall are you anyway?" He grinned and said, "6'2" on the inside." All I could do was laugh. He didn't know about my list. In that moment I realized I was standing in front of someone who met nearly all thirty-two requirements on my list. (I let the brown hair and green eyes pass.) Scott was 6'2" on the inside. That was all that mattered.

Love is always a risk. Anything really good usually is. Once Scott and I actually figured out that we both liked each other, we decided to pray about whether we should go out together. Scott thought this meant we were already boyfriend and girlfriend, and praying together just sealed the deal. I thought this meant that we weren't boyfriend and girlfriend and were praying about if we should be. Clearly, we were communicating brilliantly from the onset of our relationship.

This relationship was a new start. It was so different. And I wanted to be different than I had been in the past. I wanted to be sure that this was the right thing. I wanted Scott to be sure that he was sure. And I would have appreciated a sign in the heavens from God, like a meteor shower spelling out the words, "Yes, Sue, you can go out with Scott. Love, Jesus." Because I wanted some guarantees. I also would have liked a written contract from Scott stating that he actually liked me, that he wasn't just messing with my head, and that he was going to keep liking me after the first week of dating. This was important stuff. I was scared, and I wanted to hedge my bets if I could.

I remember one particularly vulnerable talk during which I told Scott, "I really like you. And I am scared that maybe you will stop liking me." And Scott, in all of his aged wisdom (he is two years and a day older than me), took my hand and said, "Sue, either we are going to go out and get married. Or we are going to go out and break up. Those are the two options. And I really like you, too." I *really* enjoyed him holding my hand. It made it hard to concentrate on his words. But what he was saying made sense. We liked each other. And now we were just going to have to take the risk of having our hearts broken if we wanted to figure out if "like" might turn into love.

I had this unspeakable dream of being loved. Of being loveable. And being wanted. And here was this fine, funny man that was ready to make my dream a reality. But I was going to have to let go of my fear. I was going to have to be brave. And I was going to have to trust Scott, in all of his 6'2"-on-the-inside goodness, hoping against hope that love would save the day. Was I going to say, "No thanks. I'm not friends with boys," or was I going to say, "Yes, I would like you to be my boyfriend"? He loved Jesus and was super cute and funny. So I risked it. What can I say?

What I can say is that in that moment, hope bloomed. I recognized that God was on the move in my life and my heart. And I wanted in on what He had for me. Even if it meant not going to New York for an internship. Even if it meant liking a boy without a written contract. I wasn't the same girl who had made dumb relationship choices before. Scott was not like the other boys I had liked who treated me like I didn't matter. He was different. Also, let's be honest, I was really hoping that Scott would kiss me. And in the way that only God can, He used my own hopes and dreams—the ones He placed inside of me—to heal my heart. He used Scott to reveal His love for me. He showed me that a man could be trusted. And when I married Scott two years later, it sealed the deal. Hope won out.

I don't know what my life would be like right now if Scott and I hadn't risked our hearts to find out if we were meant to be together. But I can tell you what has happened since we took that risk. I am more of who

I was meant to become. Scott is more of who he was meant to become. We have three boys—Jack, Will, and Addison—who light us up with joy and have turned our world inside out. We have lived out a crazy church-planting adventure together and have a church family whom we love and who love us back. We have had a lot of struggles, some dark moments, and some wildness. And we have had almost twenty years of laughing every day together. Of holding hands. Of kisses. And of deciding every day to keep on loving each other. It's not always easy. It doesn't always look pretty. But it is good. So good.

We take risks together. We fight off fear. And we believe that God is who He says He is and that He will do what He says He will do. He is our hope. We are singing His song. We don't get it right every time. We make mistakes and have to hit our knees daily. But we know that the God of the Universe has us in the palm of His hand. He is calling us to dream bigger dreams. And we are saying yes. And each time we say yes, hope grows.

Lord save us all from old age and broken health and a hope tree that has lost the faculty of putting out blossoms.

Mark Twain

Growing Hope

I don't have the greenest thumb. Plants that I long to grow often die within a week. But there are these juniper bushes in front of my house that I abhor and that I am sure will outlive me. I never water them, and I try to ignore them. But they are hanging right in there. They are serious bushes. Evergreen, very hearty, and so poky. Every time I trim them, I want to yank them out. But I know that it took my parents a very sturdy chain and a huge pickup to yank out their junipers. So I haven't even tried. But they will not die. Their roots are so deeply dug in that they are immovable. A few years ago I hacked a tiny rose bush out of the middle of the junipers. They had completely taken it over. And now looking at the junipers, I couldn't tell you where the rose bush was. It has filled in any holes with its thick bushy greenness.

It says in Proverbs that "hope deferred makes the heart sick, but a longing fulfilled is a tree of life." I wonder if it was referencing a juniper tree. It's not unthinkable. Juniper trees are found in the Middle East. They need little water or maintenance. They are sought after in the desert for shelter and used as protection against the wind. Elijah rested under a juniper tree when he was ministered to by angels. The juniper is resilient and long living. Its root system is undeniably strong. It is a bush that begs you to think twice before tackling it. It just won't quit.

The juniper is the perfect visual for a hope tree. We want the kind of hope that flourishes in the desert. Hope that keeps on growing no matter what life throws its way. Hope that offers shade and wind resistance and provides a place to be restored. We need its roots solidly established in the love of Christ, sending out new hope blossoms every day. We want a hope that overtakes everything in its path. As we move forward on our faith adventure into all that God has for us, the joy and pain, the triumphs and trials, the peaks and valleys, we want tough hope.

Against all hope, Abraham in hope believed and so became the father of many nations, just as it had been said to him, "So shall your offspring be."

Romans 4:18 NIV

The Hopeful

Abraham was the father of tough hope. He shouldn't have had any at all. He was old. Sarah was old. How in the world could he believe that God would give him a child? Against all hope. He, in hope, believed. He believed in hope. Even when it seemed foolish. Even when it didn't make any sense. He risked everything for the God who loved him most of all. And he believed that one day he would be a father. Because God said so. The crazy thing was that hope worked. God moved on Abraham's behalf. *Abraham in hope believed and so became the father of many nations.* The impossible was achieved because Abraham believed and so became. This is a hallmark of the hopeful. The crest of those with tough hope. We believe that God is who He says He is. And that He will do what He says He will do. We risk more. We dream bigger. We fear less. Because of hope.

Life is either a daring adventure or nothing at all.

Helen Keller

Let the Adventure Begin

With our roots dug deep into the truth of who God is, the impossible is possible. God wants us to risk everything for the love of Him. He wants us to throw off fear and dive into the knowledge that He is holding us completely in the palm of His hand. He wants us to dream big dreams because He is the God without limits. He is sounding the call of our greatest adventure yet. He is calling us to be a part of Abraham's tribe: the Hopeful. To love Him with all our hearts, our souls, and our minds and to place all our hopes in Him. The more we know Him, the more we have hope. The more we see Him move in our lives, the more we have hope. The more we recognize His character, the more we have hope. He is our hope. He wants our lives to ring out with His joy and peace. There is nothing that He won't do on our behalf. On this adventure of faith, He is above all things, faithful.

We don't have to be afraid. We can use our fear as a jumping of place into faith. We can be brave. We can be more than we have ever been before. We can risk more because His love is guaranteed. We have hope because we have Jesus. In Him and through Him we find our strength, our endurance, our freedom, our redemption, our joy, our love, our comfort, our healing, our salvation, our deliverance, and the magnificent end to our story. When hope sings, the lights come on, our eyes are opened, and we are truly free. And it absolutely does not get any better than that. Ever.

Blessed are those whose help is the God of Jacob,
whose hope is in the LORD their God.
He is the Maker of heaven and earth,
the sea, and everything in them—
he remains faithful forever.

Psalms 146:5-6 NIV

CONCLUSION
Sing It Right Out

I have always been a karaoke car singer. My boys and I were in the car the other day, leaving the grocery store parking lot, when one of my favorite songs came on the radio. I love a good song. I love singing loudly. My boys just try to ignore me, which makes me sing louder. We pulled up to the intersection, and the light was red. I was in the left turn lane with a car to my right. When this song got to the chorus, I threw back my head and let loose, singing at full volume. I heard some snickering from Will and Addison in the backseat. Let them laugh. I knew the song by heart, and I knew that I sounded good. The laughing got louder.

Jack, who was sitting next to me in the passenger seat, said, "Mom, look." I turned to look at him, still singing full volume, of course, to see that he had rolled down his window. The car to our right also had their window down. Apparently, I had been giving a concert. The lady who was driving was grinning from ear to ear, trying not to look at me. But she could hear me and my beautiful vocal stylings, that was for sure.

I started laughing and turned bright red. The boys were dying laughing. They got me. Maybe this would keep me quiet. I may have died a little inside, but I kept singing anyway. A good song has to be sung. It has to be shared. And the joy of it is infectious. I'm not sure if the lady in the car next to me was laughing at me or with me, but either way, I know that she had a moment of joy because of that song.

Hope is a song that needs to be sung loudly. In this world. In this time. In this moment. With the darkness closing in, there are so many people who don't have anything to hope for. They don't have anyone to trust in. They don't know the joy and peace and grace that they were created for. They are sitting in the dark waiting for the Light Bearer to come, just like you were before you knew that hope was meant for you. You have a choice. You can hold all that hope in, or you can bring the light and share it with whomever is sitting next to you.

God wants each of our journeys to end with the same destination: eternity with Him. He would like you to share His song of hope with as many people as you can. He wants you singing out daily. With your words, your actions, and the joy that lights you from within. So sing on out. And sing loud. Really loud. Embarrassingly loud. Because the God of hope is singing His love over you and all His kids. And we want everyone to get in on it, don't we?

My great hope, as you have read this book, is that you have been filled to overflowing with the hope of the One who loves you most of all. And I hope that you are bent on spreading that hope to everyone around you. I want you to be a full-fledged member of the Hopeful Tribe, ready to hope against all hope, because you know how truly awesome God truly is. You know He is able to meet every need, calm every fear, and galvanize your faith in Him. And my prayer is that you are infused with joy, realizing how much hope God truly has for you on your faith adventure. He is not holding back. And He doesn't want you to either. Keep singing with Him! Keep hoping in Him! And know that your greatest adventure is yet to come!

May the God of hope fill you with all joy and peace as you trust in him, so that you may overflow with hope by the power of the Holy Spirit.

Romans 15:13 NIV

Acknowledgments

Henry Ward Beecher said, "Gratitude is the fairest blossom which springs from the soul."

I have so much to be thankful for . . . blossoms galore! I am beyond grateful to have had the opportunity to write this book and for the people who made it possible.

Scott, Jack, Will, and Addison. Thank you for your great patience and good hugs during this project. I know it wasn't easy! I love you the most.

Mom, Dad, Erica, Jenny, and Chris. Thank you for letting me share our family's stories. I love that hope is woven through them. Three cheers for Resurrection Ruth and Resilient Richard!

Beth, Cori, Rene, and Ben. Thank you for your friendship and letting me share our stories. You have all shown me hope in how you live out your lives.

Wendy. Thank you for your belief in this book and for the long road of championing it!

Dawn Woods, Susan Cornell, and the Abingdon team. Thank you for the amazing opportunity to partner with you in writing *Hope Sings* and for all the expertise you poured into the making of it! May hope sing loudly in the hearts of many because of it!

And finally, I am grateful to Jesus. With Him, because of Him, there is hope for each of us no matter where we are in our journey of faith. For that, I am the most thankful of all.

Notes

Introduction

1. Mike Aquilina, *The Way of the Early Fathers* (Huntington, IN: Our Sunday Visitor Publishing, 2000), 554.

1: Sitting in the Dark

1. *Biographical Dictionary of Christian Missions,* ed. Gerald H. Anderson (New York: Macmillan Reference USA, 1998), s.v. "Carmichael, Amy Beatrice."

2. Amy Carmichael, *Candles in the Dark* (Fort Washington, PA: CLC Publication, 1981), 16.

2: Faith and Fear

1. William Shakespeare, *A Midsummer Night's Dream* (London: Macmillan and Company, 1877), 39.

2. Eleanor Roosevelt, *The Eleanor Roosevelt Papers Project,* George Washington University,www.gwu.edu/~erpapers/teachinger/lesson-plans/notes-er-and-ww1 .cfm. July 6, 2016.

3. Eleanor Roosevelt, *You Learn by Living* (Louisville, KY: Westminster John Knox, 1960), 29.

3: Being Brave

1. Eric Limer, "This Utterly Terrifying Glass Bridge Just Opened in China," *Popular Mechanics,* accessed July 25, 2016, www.popularmechanics.com /technology/infrastructure/a17536/shiniuzhai-glass-bridge-china/.

2. "The Kate Shelley Story," Boone County IA Genweb, accessed October 5, 2016, http://iagenweb.org/boone/history/kateshelley.htm.

4: The Big Questions

1. *Dictionary.com Unabridged*, s.v. "question," accessed July 25, 2016, www.dictionary.com/browse/question.

2. C. S. Lewis, *A Grief Observed* (New York: Harper One, 1961), 69.

7: The Hope Sing-Along

1. Tony Phillips, "NASA Spacecraft Records 'Earthsong,'" *NASA News*, accessed July 16, 2016, http://science.nasa.gov/science-news/science-at-nasa/2012/28sep_earthsong/.

9: The Redeemer

1. George Reginald Balleine, *A History of the Evangelical Party in the Church of England* (London: Longman, Greens and Company, 1908), 103.

2. Jonathan Aitkin, *John Newton* (Wheaton, IL: Crossway, 2007), 208.

12: The Story Writer

1. *Encyclopædia Britannica Online*, s.v. "Albania," accessed July 25, 2016, www.britannica.com/place/Albania.

2. *Encyclopædia Britannica Online*, s.v. "Enver Hoxha," accessed July 25, 2016, www.britannica.com/biography/Enver-Hoxha.

13: The Good Shepherd

1. Philip Keller, *A Shepherd Looks at Psalm 23* (Grand Rapids, MI: Zondervan, 1970).

Bibliography

Aitkin, Jonathan. *John Newton*. Wheaton, IL: Crossway, 2007.

Aquilina, Mike. *The Way of the Early Fathers*. Huntington, IN: Our Sunday Visitor Publishing, 2000.

Balleine, George Reginald. *A History of the Evangelical Party in the Church of England*. London: Longman, Greens and Company, 1908.

Boone County IA Genweb. "The Kate Shelley Story." Accessed October 5, 2016, http://iagenweb.org/boone/history/kateshelley.htm.

Brownley, Margaret. *Grieving God's Way*. Nashville: Thomas Nelson, 2012.

Carmichael, Amy. *Candles in the Dark*. Fort Washington, PA: CLC Publication, 1981.

———. *God's Missionary*. Fort Washington, IN: CLC Publications, 1939.

Dictionary.com Unabridged. s.v. "question." Accessed July 25, 2016, www.dictionary.com/browse/question.

Elmer, Robert. *The Duet*. Colorado Springs: Waterbrook, 2004.

Encyclopædia Britannica Online. s.v. "Albania." Accessed July 25, 2016, www.britannica.com/place/Albania.

———. s.v. "Enver Hoxha." Accessed July 25, 2016, www.britannica.com/biography/Enver-Hoxha.

Gergen, Christopher, and Gregg Vanourek. *Life Entrepreneurs*. San Francisco: Jossey-Bass, 2008.

Johnson, Joseph. "A Melody of Love." In *Carrs Lane Hymn Book*. Birmingham: Allday LTD, 1908.

Jurgens, W. A. *The Faith of the Early Fathers*. Vol. 3. Collegeville, MN: Liturgical, 1979.

Keller, Philip. *A Shepherd Looks at Psalm 23*. Grand Rapids, MI: Zondervan, 1970.

Kingsolver, Barbara. *Animal Dreams*. New York: Harper Perennial, 1990.

Lewis, C. S. *A Grief Observed*. New York: Harper One, 1961.

Limer, Eric. "This Utterly Terrifying Glass Bridge Just Opened in China." *Popular Mechanics*, accessed July 25, 2016, www.popularmechanics.com/technology/infrastructure/a17536/shiniuzhai-glass-bridge-china/.

Marstiller, James K., Jr., and Jennifer Joerding. *The Power to Innovate: Rewiring the Minds of Individuals and Organizations*. Bloomington, IN: AuthorHouse, 2005.

Morrow, Judy Gordon. *The Listening Heart*. Grand Rapids, MI: Baker, 2013.

Mumpower, Jeryl, and Warren Frederick Ilcmanh. *New York State in the Year 2000*. Albany: State University of New York Press, 1988.

Murray, Jocelyn. "Carmichael, Amy Beatrice." In *Biographical Dictionary of Christian Missions*, edited by Gerald H. Anderson. New York: Macmillan Reference USA, 1998.

Phillips, Tony. "NASA Spacecraft Records 'Earthsong.'" In *NASA News*. Accessed July 16, 2016, http://science.nasa.gov/science-news/science-at-nasa/2012/28sep_earthsong/.

Purcell, Cheralea. *Restored*. Mustang, OK: Tate, 2010.

Roosevelt, Eleanor. *The Eleanor Roosevelt Papers Project*. George Washington University, accessed July 6, 2016, www.gwu.edu/~erpapers/teachinger/lesson-plans/notes-er-and-ww1.cfm.

———*You Learn by Living*. Louisville: Westminster John Knox, 1960.

Santos, Bob. *Champions in the Wilderness*. Indiana, PA: Search for Me Ministries, 2013.

Schempf, F. Jay. *Pioneering Offshore*. Tulsa: Penwell Custom Publications, 2007.

Shakespeare, William. *A Midsummer Night's Dream*. London: Macmillan and Company, 1877.

Spurgeon, Charles Haddon. *The Sermons of the Rev. C. H. Spurgeon of London*. New York: Sheldon, Blakeman and Company, 1858.

ten Boom, Corrie. *Defeated Enemies*. Fort Washington, PA: CLC Publications, 1971.

Tozer, A. W. *Tozer for the Christian Leader*. Chicago: Moody Bible Institute, 2001.

Twain, Mark. *The Letters of Mark Twain*. Vol. 4. Fairfield, IA: First World Library, 2004.

Wade, John Donald, William E. Phipps, and Donald Davidson. *Amazing Grace in John Newton*. Macon, GA: Mercer University Press, 2001.